Colorado Mountain Hikes

Colorado Mountain Hikes

For Everyone

Routes and Maps to 105 Named Summits

Dave Muller

Quality Press
Denver, Colorado

Muller, Dave, 1935—
COLORADO MOUNTAIN HIKES FOR EVERYONE
Includes Index

Library of Congress Catalog Card Number: 87-92198
ISBN: 0-9619666-0-2

Sixth Edition
6 7 8 9

Printed in the United States of America

Front cover photo: *Grays Peak, Kelso Mountain, Torreys Peak and Grizzly Peak from Ganley Mountain.*

Back cover photo: *Sugarloaf Peak from the West Chicago Creek Campground.*

All photographs by the author

CONTENTS

CONTENTS (continued)

ACKNOWLEDGEMENTS

The assistance and encouragement of many persons were necessary for the completion of this hiking guide. My parents, Irish-American Margaret and Swiss-German Albert, nurtured me in many ways and encouraged walking. My wife, Jackie, has provided excellent home support and accompanied me on some of these hikes. My children have been special partners in my mountain explorations. My two eldest sons, Paul, who started it all by daring me to climb Pikes Peak with him, and Tom, who has made many a summit possible, deserve special mention. Mairi Hamilton Clark assisted with enthusiasm by typing the text. I am also grateful to my many hiking companions especially Tony Bianchi, Mary Brewer, S. Macon Cowles, Larry Currier, D.J. Inman, Jim Mahoney, Andrew Muller, Matthew Muller, Sara Muller, Jim Sherman and Harve Smith. Above all, I thank the Lord of the Universe who provides us with such wonderful playgrounds.

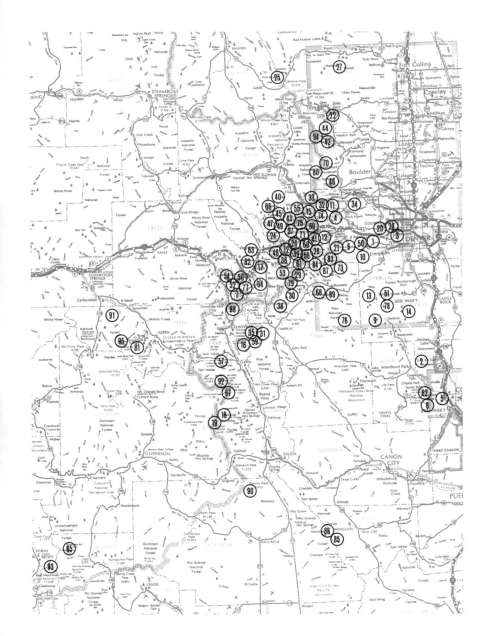

HIKE LOCATIONS

INTRODUCTION

This book describes 105 summit hikes which have either not appeared in other guides or, if described elsewhere, have lacked certain details which the author considers important. These routes are intended for a wide variety of hikers and cover peaks from six to fourteen thousand feet in height, readily accessible to remote trailheads and relatively short distances to long treks. None of the hikes are especially dangerous nor do any require ropes, pitons or other technical equipment. The beginning hiker, the newcomer to Colorado, families with children, those with certain physical limitations and even the advanced hiker, may all find routes of interest in this guidebook.

Special effort has been taken to give clear, detailed information about each hike to minimize the possibility of the reader becoming lost. From the areas and summits described, one can become more familiar with the topography of Colorado and can prospect for future outings.

Each hike description begins with certain key facts. The distance given is for one way unless a loop trip or a two summit hike is described. The time required for the hike is divided into ascent and descent times and, when applicable, time necessary between two summits. These times were required by the author (a middle aged, non-smoking "peak bagger" in good but not excellent condition), over the last six years and include brief stops of a minute or two but not significant breaks. After a few hikes the reader can determine whether to add or subtract time in future hike planning from this guide.

Starting elevation and elevation gain are self explanatory but the latter is especially important in assessing the energy required for the hike. When elevation gain is lost on the ascent or required on the descent, this will be stated.

Difficulty will be described as easy, moderate, more difficult or most difficult depending on distance, elevation gain and special challenges of the route. The hikes are presented in ascending degree of difficulty, (i.e. the easiest hike is listed first). Admittedly some of these rankings will be debatable. When two peaks are listed for one hike, the rating applies to the difficulty in reaching both summits combined.

The presence of a trail will be listed. A trail is reassuring to most hikers but some enjoy bushwhacking and the greater feelings of adventure. The use of a compass and attention to features of the terrain, especially the location of streams, creeks and lakes, will be essential when hiking without a trail. It is very easy to get lost in the Rockies.

Relevant maps for each hike will include the U.S. Geological Survey 7½ minute maps which provide the greatest detail. U.S.G.S. county maps and maps of the National Forest, when applicable, cover a greater area but are less detailed. Each hike description will be accompanied by a map reproduction usually of the appropriate county map. Maps may be obtained from the relevant governmental agency or from sporting goods stores. The main branch of the Denver Public Library carries all of the Colorado 7½ minute maps.

3

Views from each summit will be noted to enhance the pleasure of reaching the top. Only the more prominent visible landmarks will be mentioned. These will depend on the author's visibility and awareness on the day the hike occured. Directions will be based on compass readings.

A comment on each hike will mention items of historic or topographic interest. The author owes much to the many Colorado hiking and historic books which have been written and references appear at the end of the guide.

The hiking season in Colorado is generally from June through September but many of the peaks, especially those of lower elevation, will be accessible over a longer period.

SOME DEFINITIONS:

Bushwhack means to walk through forest, field, undersbrush and marsh without benefit of trail. A cairn is a pile of stones used as a marker. Couloir refers to a steep indentation on the side of a mountain. A gulch is a narrow ravine created originally by the drainage of water. Scree refers to a steep collection of loose, small rock and gravel on the mountainside. Talus is a mass of mountain rocks which are larger and more fixed than scree but not as large as boulders. Tundra refers to grassy, treeless areas at higher mountain elevations.

RECOMMENDED EQUIPMENT:

Boots with good tread and ankle support are especially important in crossing rocks and are always advised. Area maps, a backpack with compass, flashlight, survival blanket, rain protection, warm extra clothing, including a sweater, adequate food and especially water are also necessary. A lack of food can be endured for some time but to run out of water can be most unpleasant and even life threatening since dehydration frequently occurs with extra exertion at high altitudes. Carry at least a quart and a half of water per person for a half day hike. An ice axe will be helpful in fields of snow, ice or scree. Know how to use the ice axe as a brake if you begin to slide on these surfaces. A climbing helmet is not required for any hike in this guidebook but can protect you from the ever present danger of falling rock and can lessen injury if you should fall.

Any book of hiking routes cannot free the user from the need for good judgement in the conduct of the hike. Even a minor fall on rock can be very injurious and weather conditions can change rapidly and transform an easy route into a very difficult one.

The author hopes that these hike descriptions can assist the reader with many enjoyable and informative trips into the wonderful Colorado mountains.

MOUNTAIN ELEVATIONS

Hike Number	Mountain	Elevation
23	Green Mountain	6855 feet or 2089 meters
20	Mount Zion (Jefferson County)	7059 feet or 2152 meters
5	Mount Cutler	7200 feet or 2195 meters
20	Lookout Mountain	7560 feet or 2304 meters
10	The Brother	7810 feet or 2380 meters
3	Mount Falcon	7851 feet or 2393 meters
13	Baldy Peak	7872 feet or 2399 meters
9	Cheesman Mountain	7933 feet or 2418 meters
51	Raleigh Peak	8183 feet or 2494 meters
1	Genesee Mountain	8284 feet or 2525 meters
78	Long Scraggy Peak	8812 feet or 2686 meters
62	Rocky Mountain	9250 feet or 2819 meters
62	Mount Manitou	9460 feet or 2883 meters
8	Saint Peters Dome	9690 feet or 2954 meters
50	Bergen Peak	9708 feet or 2959 meters
2	Ormes Peak	9727 feet or 2965 meters
14	Devils Head	9748 feet or 2971 meters
22	Lily Mountain	9786 feet or 2983 meters
27	West White Pine Mountain	10,305 feet or 3141 meters
42	Horsetooth Peak	10,344 feet or 3153 meters
34	Tremont Mountain	10,388 feet or 3166 meters
11	Fairburn Mountain	10,390 feet or 3167 meters
17	Royal Mountain	10,502 feet or 3201 meters
12	Alps Mountain	10,560 feet or 3219 meters
4	Fox Mountain	10,921 feet or 3329 meters
44	Estes Cone	11,006 feet or 3355 meters
31	Round Hill	11,243 feet or 3427 meters
6	Squaw Mountain	11,486 feet or 3501 meters
41	Griffith Mountain	11,568 feet or 3526 meters
54	Hornsilver Mountain	11,572 feet or 3527 meters
25	Diamond Peaks (Highest)	11,582 feet or 3530 meters
40	Bottle Peak	11,584 feet or 3531 meters
21	Chief Mountain	11,709 feet or 3569 meters
73	Rosedale Peak	11,825 feet or 3604 meters
33	Mount Epworth	11,843 feet or 3610 meters
52	Resolution Mountain	11,905 feet or 3629 meters
80	Satanta Peak	11,979 feet or 3651 meters
7	Chalk Mountain	12,017 feet or 3663 meters
55	Twin Cone (northern)	12,058 feet or 3675 meters
55	Twin Cone (southern)	12,060 feet or 3676 meters
88	Mount Zion (Lake County)	12,126 feet or 3696 meters
38	Little Baldy Mountain	12,142 feet or 3701 meters
32	Kingston Peak	12,147 feet or 3702 meters
71	Pendleton Mountain	12,275 feet or 3741 meters
68	Mount Blaine	12,303 feet or 3750 meters
46	Caribou Peak	12,310 feet or 3752 meters
43	Red Mountain	12,315 feet or 3754 meters
68	North Twin Cone Peak	12,319 feet or 3755 meters
89	South Twin Cone Peak	12,323 feet or 3756 meters
28	Geneva Mountain	12,335 feet or 3760 meters
69	Republican Mountain	12,386 feet or 3775 meters
76	Bison Peak	12,431 feet or 3789 meters

Hike Number	Mountain	Elevation
84	Kataka Mountain	12,441 feet or 3792 meters
83	Bandit Peak	12,444 feet or 3793 meters
47	Mount Trelease	12,477 feet or 3803 meters
15	Colorado Mines Peak	12,493 feet or 3808 meters
60	Sugarloaf Peak	12,513 feet or 3814 meters
82	Uneva Peak	12,522 feet or 3817 meters
77	Corbett Peak	12,583 feet or 3835 meters
30	Mount Volz	12,589 feet or 3837 meters
66	Bills Peak	12,703 feet or 3872 meters
49	Mount Bethel	12,705 feet or 3872 meters
67	Birthday Peak	12,730 feet or 3880 meters
24	Coon Hill	12,757 feet or 3888 meters
58	Otter Mountain	12,766 feet or 3891 meters
63	Buffalo Mountain	12,777 feet or 3894 meters
80	Mount Neva	12,814 feet or 3906 meters
29	Glacier Peak	12,853 feet or 3918 meters
88	Buckeye Peak	12,867 feet or 3922 meters
87	Mount Logan	12,871 feet or 3923 meters
74	Breckinridge Peak	12,889 feet or 3929 meters
36	Revenue Mountain	12,889 feet or 3929 meters
16	South Peak	12,892 feet or 3929 meters
71	Ganley Mountain	12,902 feet or 3933 meters
37	Woods Mountain	12,940 feet or 3933 meters
45	Vasquez Peak	12,947 feet or 3946 meters
91	Mount Sopris	12,953 feet or 3948 meters
91	West Mount Sopris	12,953 feet or 3948 meters
64	Peak 8	12,987 feet or 3958 meters
61	Whale Peak	13,078 feet or 3986 meters
70	Paiute Peak	13,088 feet or 3989 meters
19	Fitzpatrick Peak	13,112 feet or 3997 meters
75	Robeson Peak	13,140 feet or 4005 meters
39	Kelso Mountain	13,164 feet or 4012 meters
56	Jaque Peak	13,205 feet or 4025 meters
93	Engineer Mountain	13,218 feet or 4029 meters
26	Mount Sniktau	13,234 feet or 4034 meters
90	Antora Peak	13,269 feet or 4044 meters
85	Comanche Peak	13,277 feet or 4047 meters
86	Venable Peak	13,334 feet or 4064 meters
75	Engelmann Peak	13,362 feet or 4073 meters
81	Mount Buckskin	13,370 feet or 4075 meters
79	Mount Guyot	13,370 feet or 4075 meters
58	Mount Wilcox	13,408 feet or 4087 meters
48	Grizzly Peak	13,427 feet or 4093 meters
57	Quail Mountain	13,461 feet or 4103 meters
94	Pagoda Mountain	13,497 feet or 4114 meters
18	Emma Burr Mountain	13,538 feet or 4126 meters
65	Matterhorn Peak	13,590 feet or 4142 meters
53	Bald Mountain	13,684 feet or 4171 meters
35	Mount Sheridan	13,748 feet or 4190 meters
92	Iowa Peak	13,831 feet or 4216 meters
59	Horseshoe Mountain	13,898 feet or 4237 meters
95	Capitol Peak	14,130 feet or 4307 meters
72	Torreys Peak	14,267 feet or 4349 meters
72	Grays Peak	14,270 feet or 4349 meters

1. Genesee Mountain 8,284 feet

Hike Distance: 0.3 miles each way
Hiking Time: Up in 12 minutes. Down in 8 minutes.
Starting Elevation: 7,980 feet
Elevation Gain: 304 feet
Difficulty: Easy
Trail: Partial
Relevant Maps: Evergreen 7½ minute
Jefferson County Number One

Views from the summit: E to Denver
SSE to Long Scraggy Peak and Pikes Peak
SE to Mount Morrison
SW to Mount Evans

Comment:

This hike lies within area designated a Denver Mountain Park. A group of buffalo graze in a large enclosure on the north flank of Genesee Mountain. A local group of the Daughters of the American Revolution has placed a new flag on the summit flagpole on every Flag Day since 1911.

Directions to the trailhead:

Using Exit 254 drive south from Interstate 70. Turn right after a few hundred yards into Genesee Trail Road which winds for 2.5 miles to road end just below the summit. Drive 1.1 miles from I-70 up this road and park in the clear area on your right (west).

The Hike:

Follow a trail leading up and northwest past picnic tables and cross the road which has continued its winding ascent past where you parked. Continue up in a west northwesterly direction to a large flagpole on the top. Trees obscure some of the views to the north and west. Return to the east southeast as you ascended.

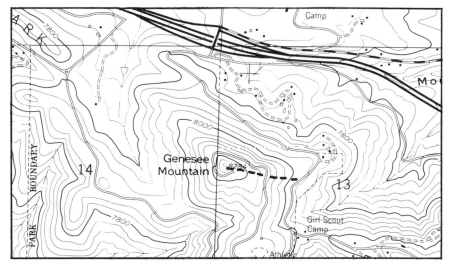

2. Ormes Peak 9,727 feet

Hike Distance: 0.3 miles each way
Hiking Time: Up in 22 minutes. Down in 8 minutes.
Starting Elevation: 9,320 feet
Elevation Gain: 407 feet
Difficulty: Easy
Trail: Intermittent and faint
Relevant Maps: Cascade 7½ minute, Woodland Park 7½ minute.
                    El Paso County Number One
                    Pike National Forest
Views from the summit: NE to Air Force Academy
                    NW to Rampart Reservoir
                    ENE to Blodgett Peak
                    S to Sheep Mountain
                    SE to Colorado Springs and Cheyenne Mountain
                    SW to Pikes Peak

Comment:

This mountain is named after the father of Robert M. Ormes, the editor of the frequently revised *Guide to the Colorado Mountains*. The elder Ormes mapped some of the area and was a leader of a local climbing group.

Directions to the trailhead:

From Colorado Springs drive northwest from I-25 on U.S. 24 for 17.8 miles to the town of Woodland Park. At Baldwin Street, where a sign welcomes the visitor to Woodland Park, turn right (northwest). Baldwin becomes a street called Rampart Range Road and also Teller County Road 22. Take this street for 2.95 miles from U.S. 24 to an intersection with Loy Creek Road. Turn right on Loy Creek Road and ascend the canyon for 1.5 miles to a 4 way intersection. Turn right (south) onto the real Rampart Range Road which is unpaved. Go southwest on the Rampart Range Road for 6.1 miles to a turn-off to the east which is road 303. Follow this road east for 0.95 miles to another fork. Take the right fork which is road 302. Take this road east for 1.35 miles and park off the road on the left (north). From the south, access is via the Rampart Range Road which begins in the southwest corner of the Garden of the Gods, 0.1 miles east of Balanced Rock. To reach the turnoff onto road 303 drive north on Rampart Range Road for 15.15 miles. Regular cars should have no problem reaching the trailhead by either route.

The Hike:

Proceed up and due north through the sparse trees. A faint trail is intermittent to the top but the hike is easily done without any trail. The unmarked summit lies at the northwestern edge of a relatively flat area. The view of Pikes Peak from here is extraordinary. Return by the ascent route.

Pikes Peak from Ormes Peak

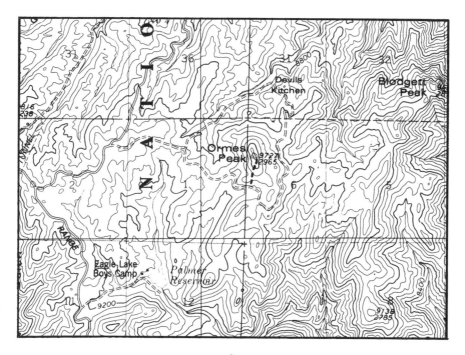

3. Mount Falcon 7,851 feet

Hike Distance: 0.66 miles each way
Hiking Time: Up in 20 minutes. Down in 15 minutes.
Starting Elevation: 7,780 feet
Elevation Gain: 231 feet (includes 80 feet of extra elevation gain each way)
Difficulty: Easy
Trail: All the way
Relevant Maps: Morrison 7½ minute
Jefferson County Number One
Mount Falcon Park Map (Jefferson County Open Space).

Views from the summit: NNE to Mount Morrison, Red Rocks Park and
Green Mountain
NE to Denver
NW to James Peak
SW to Mount Evans
WNW to Chief Mountain and Squaw Mountain

Comment:

Mount Falcon was named by John Brisben Walker, a successful entrepreneur who died in 1931 at the age of 84. Walker had a doctor of philosophy degree from Georgetown University in Washington, D.C. He brought Cosmopolitan magazine into prominence and established Red Rocks Park. He hoped to build a mansion for himself and also a summer White House for the U.S. President near the top of Mount Falcon. The home ruins are located a half mile north of the summit and the summer White House ruins are one mile northeast of the summit tower.

Directions to the trailhead:

Drive either south from Colorado Road 74 at Kittredge on the Meyers Gulch Road for 2.9 miles or north from U.S. 285 on the Parmalee Gulch Road for 2.75 miles. (The Parmalee Gulch Road goes north from 285 in Turkey Creek Canyon east of Conifer and west of the Evergreen cutoff. This road becomes the Meyers Gulch Road before it reaches Colorado 74). Turn east on Picutis Road and make a quick left turn onto Comanche Road. After 0.1 miles, make a right onto Oh Kay Road and after another 0.1 miles turn right onto Picutis Road. After 0.45 more miles turn left onto Nambe Road and drive 1.3 miles further to road end at the Mount Falcon Park parking area.

The Hike:

The trailhead is evident at the southeastern corner of the parking area and is well marked. Continue southeast past picnic tables and toilet facilities for 0.3 miles to a fork. Turn right and continue to the south on the Tower Trail which also leads to the Eagles Eye Shelter. After another 0.1 mile on the Tower Trail is another fork. Keep right and stay on the Tower Trail, ascend some stone steps and in 0.26 more miles the summit and overlying wooden lookout tower are reached. The most direct descent route is to backtrack on the route just described. However if you wish to take a longer loop trail back to your vehicle and perhaps explore the park, there are several possible trails on the Mount Falcon Park map.

Walker Home ruins on Mount Falcon

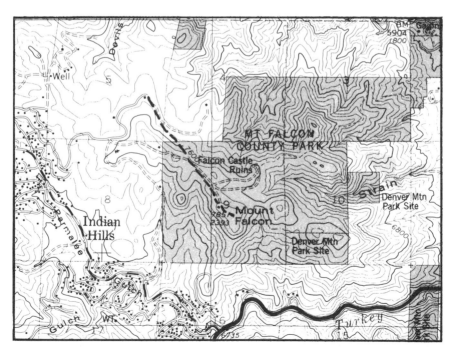

4. Fox Mountain 10,921 feet

Hike Distance: 0.65 miles each way
Hiking Time: Up in 25 minutes. Down in 15 minutes.
Starting Elevation: 10,470 feet
Elevation Gain: 451 feet
Difficulty: Easy (easy hand work necessary around the summit).
Trail: To Saint Marys Lake
Relevant Maps: Empire 7½ minute
                    Clear Creek County
                    Arapaho National Forest
Views from the summit: NW to St. Marys Glacier
                    ESE to Silver Lake
                    SSE to Mount Evans
                    SE to Squaw Mountain, Papoose Mountain and
                    Chief Mountain and Lake Quivira
                    SSW to Square Top Mountain
                    SW to Grays Peak and Torreys Peak
                    W to St. Marys Lake

Comment:

St. Marys Glacier is located above the north end of St. Marys Lake. It is actually an icefield rather than a glacier and is approximately ten acres wide.

Directions to the trailhead:

Drive west of Idaho Springs on I-70 for about two miles and turn off on Exit 238 and go north on Fall River Road (which is designated Road 275), for 9.7 miles to a right turning curve off the paved road. Turn left at this curve and drive north northwest on the dirt road with Silver Lake on your right (east) for 0.2 miles to a four-way intersection and park off the road. Regular cars can come this far.

The Hike:

Proceed south up an old mining road for about 10 minutes to a bend in the road toward the north. Follow a trail which passes to the west on the north side of the creek. In another seven minutes you will arrive at St. Marys Lake. From the eastern margin of the lake leave the trail and bushwhack east up over mostly talus to the top of Fox Mountain. Some easy hand work is necessary near the summit which consists of 3 rocky knobs on a rocky mesa. Descend via the ascent route.

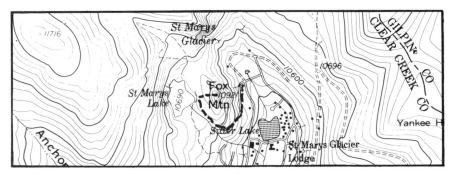

5. Mount Cutler 7,200 feet

Hike Distance: 1.0 miles each way
Hiking Time: Up in 23 minutes. Down in 20 minutes.
Starting Elevation: 6,785 feet
Elevation Gain: 427 feet (includes 6 feet extra each way)
Difficulty: Easy
Trail: All the way
Relevant Maps: Manitou Springs 7½ minute
El Paso County Number One
Pike National Forest
North Cheyenne Canon Park (Colorado Springs Park & Recreation Department)
Views from the summit: N to North Cheyenne Canyon
NE to Colorado Springs
S to Seven Falls
SSE to Cheyenne Mountain
SSW to St. Peters Dome
WNW to Mays Peak

Comment:

This mountain is named after Henry Cutler, a Massachusetts man who gave large amounts of money to Colorado College in its early years. This hiking area lies within a Colorado Springs Park. Several other trails, waterfalls and picnic areas can also be found within the park. This particular hike will usually be free of snow and ice between April and November.

Directions to the trailhead:

At the southern part of Colorado Springs drive south from Interstate 25 via Exit 140B onto South Tejon Street for 0.4 miles. Then turn right on Cheyenne Boulevard and proceed southwest for 2.5 miles to an intersection with Evans Avenue, the entrance to Seven Falls (fee area) and a sign to mark the beginning of North Cheyenne Canyon. Drive up the scenic and paved North Cheyenne Canyon Road for 1.5 more miles to a parking area on the left (south) side of the road and a Mount Cutler trail sign. Park here.

The Hike:

Follow the clear trail up and southeast as it curls to the unmarked and tree covered top of Mount Cutler. En route to the top, there are good overlooks of Seven Falls to the south. Descend as you came up.

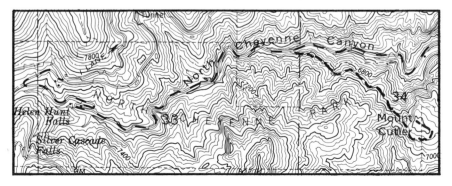

6. Squaw Mountain 11,486 feet

Hike Distance: 0.6 miles each way
Hiking Time: Up in 27 minutes. Down in 21 minutes.
Starting Elevation: 10,960 feet
Elevation Gain: 526 feet
Difficulty: Easy
Trail: All the way
Relevant Maps: Idaho Springs 7½ minute
                  Squaw Pass 7½ minute
                  Clear Creek County
                  Arapaho National Forest

Views from the summit: NNW to South Arapaho Peak, Longs Peak and
                  Mount Meeker
                  E to Denver
                  ESE to Mount Judge
                  SSE to Meridian Hill
                  SSW to Bandit Peak, Rosedale Peak and Rosalie
                  Peak
                  SE to Pikes Peak
                  SW to Mount Evans, Grays Peak and Torreys Peak
                  W to Papoose Mountain and Chief Mountain
                  WNW to James Peak

Comment:

Squaw Mountain with its bare area on the north flank can usually be clearly seen from Denver. The summit is easily accessible and affords excellent vistas from its lookout tower.

Directions to the trailhead:

Drive west from Bergen Park on Colorado 103 for 12.85 miles and turn left (southeast) on the dirt road. Drive mostly east and up on this road until a barrier blocks further vehicular traffic after 0.9 miles from Colorado 103. Park off the road.

The Hike:

Proceed northeast on the road past the barrier. The road makes several curves as it ascends. Take the right fork in the road near the top and hike directly toward the lookout tower. A good trail begins at a wooden pole at the edge of a turnaround area at road end. Take the trail northeast and then east for the last 300 feet to the summit lookout tower. Descend by the same route.

Squaw Mountain Lookout Tower

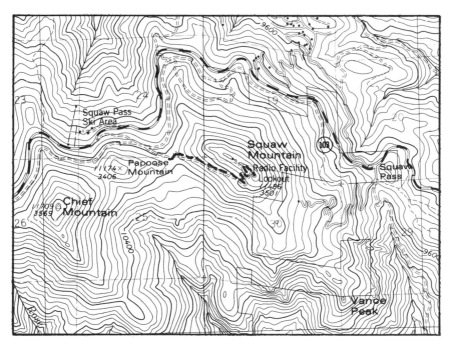

7. Chalk Mountain 12,017 feet

Hike Distance:	0.8 miles each way
Hiking Time:	Up in 30 minutes. Down in 22 minutes.
Starting Elevation:	11,316 feet (Fremont Pass)
Elevation Gain:	701 feet
Difficulty:	Easy
Trail:	Initial 25%
Relevant Maps:	Climax 7½ minute
	Lake County
	San Isabel National Forest

Views from the summit: NNE to Copper Mountain
NNW to Jaque Peak
NW to Sheep Mountain
E to Amax Mine and Bartlett Mountain
ESE to Mount Sherman
SSE to Mount Arkansas
SE to Mount Democrat
SW to Buckeye Peak
W to Mount of the Holy Cross

Comment:

In 1936 a ski area with a double rope tow was begun on Chalk Mountain and continued for a few years. For such a short hike, the vistas from the top are exceptional. The Chalk Mountain summit lies on the Continental Divide. Fremont Pass is named after the explorer, General John C. Fremont.

Directions to the trailhead:

Drive to Fremont Pass on Colorado 91 at the Climax mining area between Leadville and Copper Mountain. Park on the west side of the pass.

The Hike:

Proceed west and then north on a dirt road for a hundred yards, fork left and ascend more steeply. After a quarter mile from the trailhead leave the road and follow an overgrown trail up to the west. At three quarters of a mile from the trailhead, you will reach a ridge and fifty yards farther a rock pile on the flat summit. Enjoy the fine views and return by the ascent route.

Amax Mine from Chalk Mountain

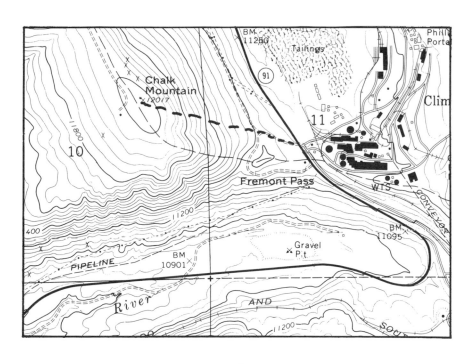

8. St. Peters Dome 9,690 feet

Hike Distance: 0.6 miles each way
Hiking Time: Up in 26 minutes. Down in 18 minutes.
Starting Elevation: 9,278 feet
Elevation Gain: 442 feet (Includes 15 feet of extra elevation gain near the top each way).
Difficulty: Easy (but some easy hand work and route finding are required near the top).
Trail: Most of the way. Vague around the top.
Relevant Maps: Mount Big Chief 7½ minute
                   El Paso County Number Three
                   Pike National Forest
Views from the summit: NNE to Mount Cutler and Colorado Springs
                   ENE to Cheyenne Mountain
                   S to the trailhead
                   W to Mount Rosa
                   WNW to Pikes Peak

Comment:

This used to be a popular hike with wooden stairs for the final ascent to the summit. Some of the wood from these steps can be found near the top. The final part of this hike requires some caution since the route gets obscure near the top. The rocky summit projection to the north is designated St. Peters Dome. The southern rocky projection probably requires a technical ascent. This hike also involves the lovely and historic Gold Camp Road which connects Colorado Springs with Cripple Creek.

Directions to the trailhead:

In west Colorado Springs from the intersection of the Cheyenne Zoo Road and Cheyenne Boulevard, drive west up the Old Stage Road for 6.8 miles and join the Gold Camp Road. Turn left, proceed nine tenths of a mile and park on the right at the trailhead and a road junction. This point can also be reached by the Gold Camp Road from the west. Regular cars can reach this trailhead from either direction.

The Hike:

Proceed left (north northwest) and up the initially gradual trail. In about 12 minutes the trail becomes faint. Continue counterclockwise over rocks with some loss of elevation as you pick your way around to a saddle between two rocky summits. Find your way up the left (eastern) flank to the summit on your left (north). At the top is a metal sign and some embedded metal poles with hand wires for safety. Return the same way you ascended.

Looking south from St. Peters Dome summit

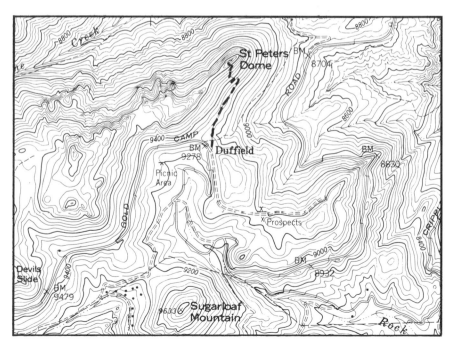

9. Cheesman Mountain 7,933 feet

Hike Distance: 0.8 miles each way
Hiking Time: Up in 34 minutes. Down in 26 minutes.
Starting Elevation: 7,180 feet
Elevation Gain: 853 feet (includes 100 feet of extra elevation gain on the ridge en route to and from the summit)
Difficulty: Easy. (Some easy hand work may be needed approaching the initial false summit.)
Trail: None
Relevant Maps: Cheesman Lake 7½ minute
                   Jefferson County Number Two
                   Pike National Forest
Views from the summit: N to Little Scraggy Peak
                   NNE to Long Scraggy Peak
                   NNW to Green Mountain
                   E to Devils Head
                   S to Cheesman Reservoir
                   SE to Thunder Butte and Pikes Peak
                   WNW to Sugarloaf Peak and Buffalo Peak

Comment:

Named after Walter S. Cheesman, a Denver businessman around the turn of the century, this peak can be reached even into November. The reservoir to the south also carries the same name and was formed by construction of the dam between 1900 and 1905.

Directions to the trailhead:

From U.S. 285 at Pine Junction drive south on Jefferson County Road 126 through Buffalo Creek for a total of 22.5 miles. Turn right onto a dirt road which passes up and west for 2.1 miles to a fork (the right fork goes to Lost Valley Ranch in 7 miles, and the left to Cheesman Reservoir in .72 miles). Park near this fork.

The Hike:

Hike up and east to a rather steep false summit and a ridge which leads to the top. Some easy use of hands may be needed in reaching this ridge. Once on the ridge, continue northeast skirting another false summit on its south side to the true summit, a huge boulder, which is unclimbable, except with technical assistance. Some wires extend downward from its top but do not appear safe. Two U.S.G.S. markers are present on the eastern edge of a rocky mesa adjacent to the summit boulder. Return by your ascent route.

Cheesman Mountain summit boulder

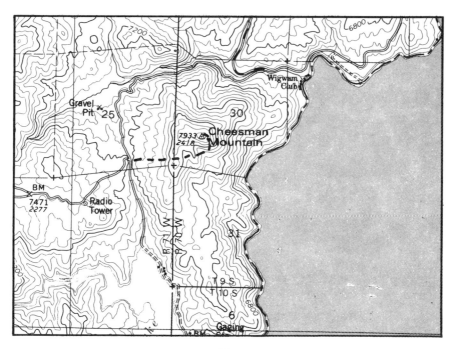

10. The Brother 7,810 feet

Hike Distance: 0.7 miles on the ascent. 1.5 miles on the descent (loop).
Hiking Time: Up in 21 minutes. Down in 38 minutes (loop).
Starting Elevation: 7,480 feet
Elevation Gain: 465 feet (includes 135 extra feet)
Difficulty: Easy
Trail: All the way
Relevant Maps: Evergreen 7½ minute
                    Jefferson County Number One
                    Alderfer-Three Sisters Park Map
                      (Jefferson County)
Views from the summit: NNW to Three Sisters
                    NE to Mount Morrison
                    NW to Bergen Peak and Elephant Butte
                    SSW to Evergreen Mountain
                    WSW to Mount Evans
                    WNW to Chief Mountain

Comment:

This hike is part of the Alderfer-Three Sisters Park in Jefferson County Open Space. There is no park fee. The trails are well marked; dogs must be kept on leash and motor vehicles are forbidden on the trails.

Directions to the trailhead:

At the center of Evergreen from the intersection of Colorado 74 and Jefferson County Road 73, drive south southwest for six tenths of a mile on Jefferson 73. Then turn right onto Buffalo Park Road and drive on this paved road for 1.3 miles and park on the right at the trailhead parking area.

The Hike:

Begin up the trail to the left of the signboard north northwest. Within fifty yards continue straight (north northeast) at a four-way intersection on the Sisters Trail. After another 120 yards, turn left onto the Ponderosa Trail and begin your clockwise loop. Ascend three tenths of a mile to a ridge and turn right onto the Brothers Lookout Trail which rises in two tenths of a mile to the rocky summit and a benchmark. Enjoy the good views before returning to the last fork at the ridge. To continue the loop, descend seventy-five yards to the right and take the right fork onto the Sisters Trail which circles back one mile to where your loop began. En route to this point stay on the Sisters Trail and avoid the Hidden Fawn Trail. From the loop onset point descend south for two tenths of a mile back to the trailhead.

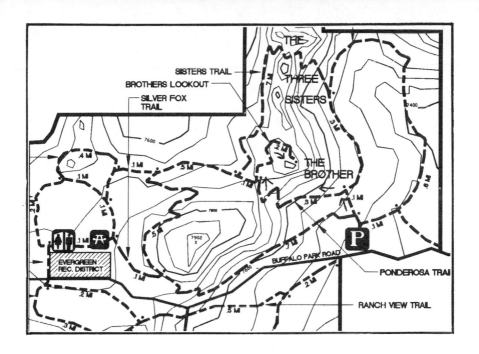

11. Fairburn Mountain 10,390 feet

Hike Distance: 1.1 miles each way
Hiking Time: Up in 45 minutes. Down in 35 minutes.
Starting Elevation: 9,310 feet
Elevation Gain: 1130 feet (includes 25 feet of extra elevation gain each
                   way between false and true summits).
Difficulty: Easy
Trail: None
Relevant Maps: Central City 7½ minute
                   Gilpin County
                   Arapaho National Forest
Views from the summit: W to James Peak and Byers Peak
                   SW to Mount Evans and Torreys Peak

Comment:

This hike will provide basic practice with the compass since there is no trail. Try this one from May until October to avoid snow underfoot.

Directions to the trailhead:

This hike begins at the Cold Springs Campground north of Central City off of Colorado 119. The campground entrance is 0.1 miles southwest of the intersection of Colorado 119 and Colorado 46 or 5.2 miles north of the intersection of Colorado 119 and Colorado 279. Drive northwest into the

23

campground for 0.8 miles and park near where a creek, flowing from the north, crosses the dirt campground road.

The Hike:

Proceed north keeping the creek to your left. Quickly you reach a large clearing with excellent views to the south and southwest. Continue upward to the north and traverse a false summit en route to a small rock cairn at the tree covered summit. The views are partial and to the west. Descend to the south approximating your ascent route.

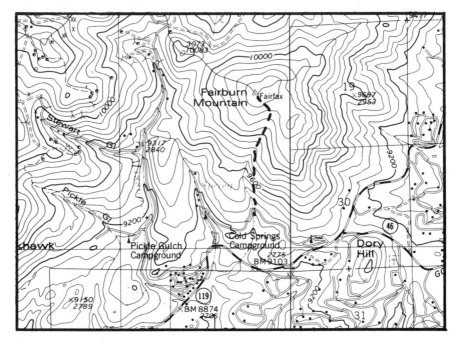

12. Alps Mountain 10,560 feet

Hike Distance: 0.45 miles each way
Hiking Time: Up in 30 minutes. Down in 16 minutes.
Starting Elevation: 9,940 feet
Elevation Gain: 620 feet
Difficulty: Easy
Trail: Initial two thirds
Relevant Maps: Idaho Springs 7½ minute
                    Clear Creek County
                    Arapaho National Forest
Views from the summit: NNW to Kingston Peak
                    NW to James Peak
                    S to Mount Evans
                    SE to Squaw Mountain and Chief Mountain
                    SW to Sugarloaf Peak, Grays Peak and Torreys Peak

24

Comment:

The area of this hike is honeycombed with old mines and their roads. This is a good outing for beginners and for early season conditioning. The route should be free of snow at least between June and October.

Directions to the trailhead:

From Interstate 70 in Idaho Springs drive southwest on Colorado 103 for a half mile. Turn right onto unpaved Spring Gulch Road and ascend 4.3 miles to a 4-way intersection and park. En route to this point drive parallel to the small creek on your left. Keep right at mile 1.6, left at mile 1.75, straight at mile 2.1 and at mile 2.5, left at mile 2.6, right at mile 3.0 and again at mile 3.9, left at mile 4.0 and again left at mile 4.1. Regular cars can reach this trailhead.

The Hike:

Proceed southeast up the road on your left. The road curves south and in a quarter mile you will arrive at a restored old cabin. Take the left fork above the cabin and continue southwest and west. Thirty yards past the cabin take a left fork to the west southwest just before mine remnants. The trail ends in a loop within forty yards. Then bushwhack up and southwest past some diggings and an abandoned cabin on your left. Ascend west on a faint trail and then curve southwest to reach the unmarked, rocky summit at the west end of an irregular ridge. The views from the top are partially obscured by trees. Return as you ascended.

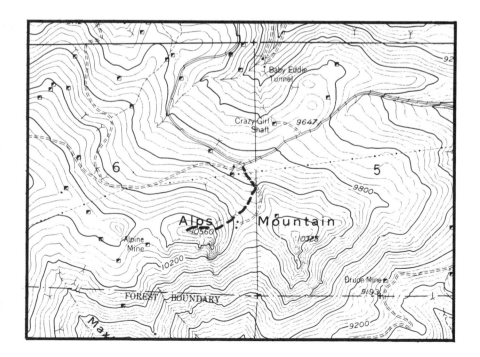

13. Baldy Peak 7,872 feet

Hike Distance: 0.8 miles each way
Hiking Time: Up in 48 minutes. Down in 34 minutes.
Starting Elevation: 6,912 feet
Elevation Gain: 960 feet
Difficulty: Easy (some easy hand work near the top).
Trail: None
Relevant Maps: Green Mountain 7½ minute
Jefferson County Number Two
Pike National Forest
Views from the summit: NNE to the Cathedral Spires
E to Long Scraggy Peak
ESE to Little Scraggy Peak
SSE to Green Mountain
SW to Redskin Mountain

Comment:

This makes a good early or late season hike with some enjoyable, easy rock hiking over the last few hundred yards to the summit. The Pike National Forest commemorates Zebulon M. Pike, an army officer, who explored various parts of the United States and was killed in the war of 1812 at the age of 34.

Directions to the trailhead:

From Pine Junction on U.S. 285 drive south on Jefferson County Road 126 for 9.8 miles. Turn right onto a paved road with a stop sign and several signs giving the distances to Redskin Group Campground (5 miles), Wellington Lake (9 miles) and Bailey (17 miles). Follow this road, which becomes unpaved, for 3.1 miles and park off the road.

The Hike:

Baldy Peak will be visible as a rocky point to the WNW. Follow an old mining road leading west from the road at a metal gate. Cross the creek and follow the old road. At a fork keep left and eventually leave the road and proceed toward the left (southwest) side of Baldy Peak. Ascend in a clockwise direction. The final ascent moves toward the northeast from the southwest. There is an easily negotiated route to the summit with a few hand holds necessary near the summit which is marked by an U.S.G.S. marker and a small pile of rocks. There are no trees to obscure the excellent panorama in every direction. Descend as you came up.

Baldy Peak looking west northwest

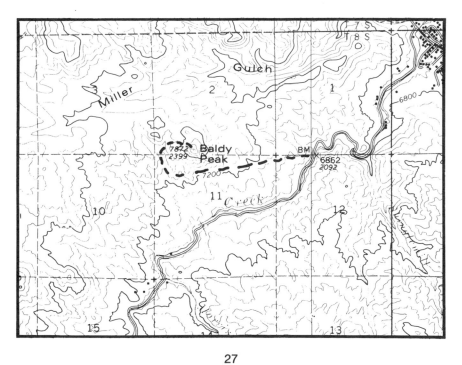

14. Devils Head 9,748 feet

Hike Distance:	1.9 miles each way
Hiking Time:	Up in 53 minutes. Down in 48 minutes.
Starting Elevation:	8,780 feet
Elevation Gain:	1,080 feet (includes an extra 112 feet)
Difficulty:	Easy
Trail:	All the way
Relevant Maps:	Devils Head 7½ minute
	Douglas County Number One
	Pike National Forest
Views from the summit:	N to Denver
	NW to Mt. Evans and Long Scraggy Peak
	SW to Cheesman Mountain
	SSE to Pikes Peak
	SSW to Thunder Butte

Comment:

This hike will usually be possible from May until November. The trailhead is reached from the Rampart Range Road which is unpaved but drivable by regular cars. This road has many side roads. Devils Head was originally called Platte Mountain until 1923. The Devils Head configuration can be seen from the southwest. The tower and cabin at the top were built by the U.S. Forest Service in 1907 and replaced in 1951 by the Army Corps of Engineers. Several informational signs and benches lie along this excellent trail.

Directions to the trailhead:

From Sedalia on US 85 (south of Denver and northwest of Castle Rock) drive west on Colorado 67 for 10.0 miles to a four-way intersection. Turn left (south) here onto the Rampart Range Road. Stay on this main road as it continues south for 9.0 miles to a fork and sign. Park here. (The right fork continues 31 miles to Woodland Park.)

The Hike:

Walk east up the left fork and reach the trailhead sign in a half mile. En route to this point keep right at two forks and avoid the campground. Ascend southeast from the trailhead sign. After a mile reach a signed fork. (The left trail leads 0.4 miles to the Zinn Memorial Overlook of Pikes Peak. A plaque at the overlook honors Commander Ralph Theodore Zinn, a 1922 graduate of the U.S. Naval Academy.) To reach Devils Head take the right fork and quickly reach a cabin and a clearing below the lookout tower, ascend the stairway to the top and the excellent views. Be careful on the steps as you retrace the ascent route back to the trailhead.

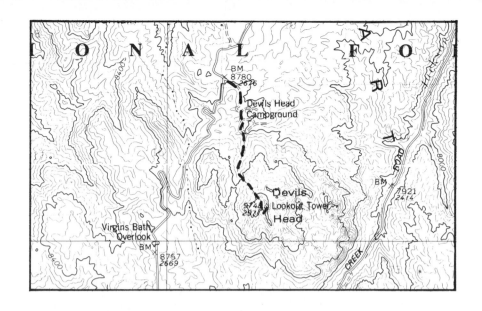

15. Colorado Mines Peak 12,493 feet

Hike Distance: 1.3 miles each way
Hiking Time: Up in 55 minutes. Down in 38 minutes.
Starting Elevation: 11,315 feet (Berthoud Pass)
Elevation Gain: 1,178 feet
Difficulty: Easy
Trail: All the way (dirt road)
Relevant Maps: Berthoud Pass 7½ minute
                   Clear Creek County
                   Arapaho National Forest
Views from the summit: NE to Mount Flora
                       E to Breckinridge Peak
                       SSW to Engelmann Peak
                       W to Berthoud Pass
                       WSW to Stanley Mountain
                       SW to Red Mountain

Comment:

Berthoud Pass is named after Edward Louis Berthoud who was born in Geneva Switzerland. Berthoud was an explorer, a faculty member at the Colorado School of Mines and at one time, President of the Colorado Central Railroad. Colorado Mines Peak lies on the Continental Divide and on the boundary between Clear Creek and Grand Counties. It was named by Neal Harr, a student at the Colorado School of Mines, in 1954.

Directions to the trailhead:

Drive on U.S. 40 either north from Empire or south from Winter Park to Berthoud Pass. Park in the area east of the pass by the restaurant and shop.

The Hike:

Proceed southeast up a well-maintained road which begins south of the pass building and winds its way to the top of Colorado Mines Peak where several buildings are located, including a large modern Mountain Bell facility. Return to Berthoud Pass via the ascent route. (A ridge walk to the northeast will reach the top of Mount Flora in 37 minutes and the Mount Eva summit, after a false summit, in 49 minutes more.)

Colorado Mines Peak from the north

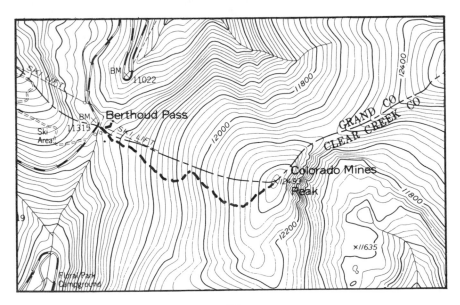

30

16. South Peak 12,892 feet

Hike Distance: 1.4 miles each way
Hiking Time: Up in 60 minutes. Down in 40 minutes.
Starting Elevation: 11,921 feet (Weston Pass)
Elevation Gain: 1,091 feet (includes 60 feet down from Weston Pass to the trail)
Difficulty: Easy
Trail: Initial 25% of the route
Relevant Maps: Mount Sherman 7½ minute
South Peak 7½ minute
Lake County
San Isabel National Forest
Views from the summit: N to Ptarmigan Peak and Weston Peak
NW to Leadville
SSW to Mount Harvard
SW to Twin Lakes
W to Mount Elbert
WNW to Mount Massive

Comment:

Weston Pass was first an indian trail and then a stage and wagon road which connected South Park with Leadville. This was a busy route until train routes were completed to Leadville from Buena Vista. At the east side of the pass lay the town of Weston which once contained several restaurants and bars to serve the traffic to the busy mining activities in California Gulch.

Directions to the trailhead:

Drive to Weston Pass which connects U.S. 285 on the east with U.S. 24 on the west. Either drive 16.2 miles to the west from U.S. 285 or 11.1 miles to the east from U.S. 24 (6.5 miles south of Leadville).This pass can be readily traversed in a regular car. Park at the summit of the pass.

The Hike:

Proceed about 200 yards west on the main Weston Pass road to an old mining road on your left which leads southwest. Follow the old road until it ends at some abandoned cabins. South Peak is visible directly ahead to the southwest with white rocky slopes leading to its summit. Cross the tundra and then some easy talus to a large rock cairn at the summit and a small radio tower nearby. Take the same route down to your car.

31

South Peak from west of Weston Pass

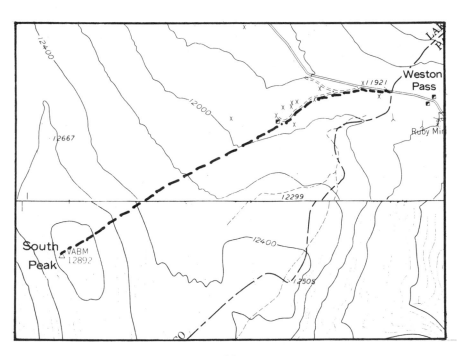

17. Royal Mountain 10,502 feet

Hike Distance: 2.0 miles each way
Hiking Time: Up in 56 minutes. Down in 38 minutes.
Starting Elevation: 9,095 feet
Elevation Gain: 1,477 feet (includes an extra 35 feet each way)
Difficulty: Easy
Trail: All the way
Relevant Maps: Frisco 7½ minute
                      Summit County Number Two
                      Arapaho National Forest – Dillon Ranger District
Views from the summit: NNW to Buffalo Mountain
                       NE to Lake Dillon
                       SE to Bald Mountain
                       WSW to Uneva Peak

Comment:

The trail to Royal Mountain passes through the ghost-town of Masontown which was settled in the 1860s by a group from the town of the same name in Pennsylvania. One hundred years later, artificial Lake Dillon was established. The first part of this hike is on the paved bike and foot path which extends from Vail to Copper Mountain, Frisco and on to Breckenridge.

Directions to the trailhead:

Drive to Main Street in Frisco. The trailhead lies on the south side of the street either 0.28 miles east of Interstate 70 or 0.8 miles west of Colorado 9. A sign states "Vail Pass—Ten Mile Canyon—National Recreational Trail." Park around this sign.

The Hike:

From the parking area walk southeast and cross Tenmile Creek on a bridge. This is the only flowing water on this hike. Go left onto the paved bikepath. After three tenths of a mile, leave the path and enter the trees on a trail to your right at a sign. Ascend south southeast and soon pass through the remnants of Masontown. Continue up and south by the right trail fork. The steep trail then reaches a fork after 1.7 miles from the trailhead. Go right (northwest) at this fork. (The other trail leads up Peak One.) After two hundred yards you reach an overlook of Tenmile Canyon and Interstate 70. Go to the right at the rockpile and follow the ridge northward to reach the high point. The views from here are partially obstructed by trees. If you want a better overlook, continue down by a faint trail to the north northeast for another quarter mile to a rocky knob. Be sure to return by your ascent route since there are steep dropoffs to the east and north.

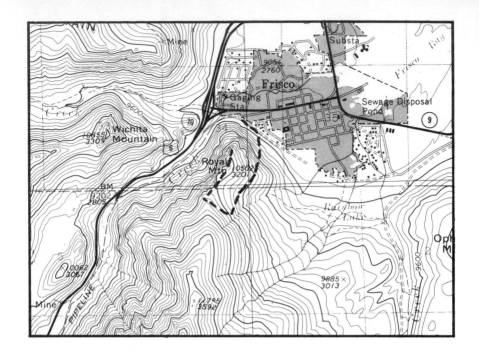

18. Emma Burr Mountain 13,538 feet

Hike Distance: 2.2 miles each way
Hiking Time: Up in 56 minutes. Down in 34 minutes.
Starting Elevation: 12,154 feet
Elevation Gain: 1,384 feet
Difficulty: Easy
Trail: From Tincup Pass part way to the summit ridge
Relevant Maps: Cumberland Pass 7½ minute
                    Gunnison County Number Five
                    Chaffee County Number Two
                    Gunnison National Forest
                    San Isabel National Forest
Views from the summit: NW to Taylor Park Reservoir
                    E to the Collegiate Peaks
                    SW to Fitzpatrick Peak and Tincup Pass
                    W to Fairview Peak

Comment:

No one seems to know how this mountain got its name. It lies on the Continental Divide and the boundaries between Chaffee and Gunnison Counties and also between the San Isabel and the Gunnison National Forests. The hike is totally above timberline with constant vistas.

34

Directions to the trailhead:

Drive to Tincup Pass. From the east drive south from the U.S. 24 east and north intersection below Buena Vista for 5.7 miles. Then turn west onto Chaffee County Road 162. Continue west on this road for a total of 16.2 miles to the historic town of Saint Elmo. Turn right in the center of town, cross a bridge and turn immediately left onto Chaffee County Road 267. This road continues for 6.3 miles up to Tincup Pass. If the snow is gone, some passenger cars can make the pass from the east. From the west Tincup Pass is reached via Cumberland Pass or Taylor Park to the town of Tincup. It is 6.7 miles east and then south from Tincup to Tincup Pass. Four wheel drive is necessary for the final three miles to the pass from Mirror Lake. Park off the road near the sign at Tincup Pass. If your car is unable to reach the pass, add the extra distances to those given for the hike as described from Tincup Pass.

The Hike:

Proceed on a blocked road which leads up and east from the road at Tincup Pass. When this road ends after a few hundred yards, angle left up over tundra to a saddle. At the saddle hike north up the ridge past a false summit to a cairn on the grassy high point. Go down as you ascended.

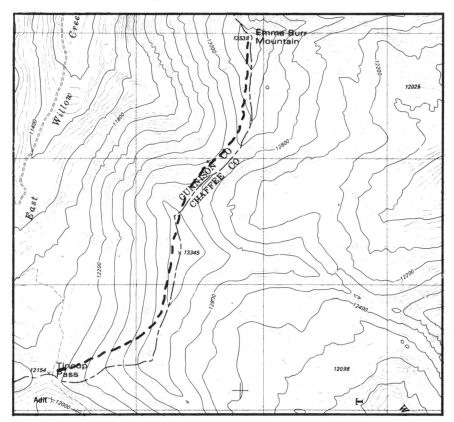

19. Fitzpatrick Peak 13,112 feet

Hike Distance: 1.35 miles each way
Hiking Time: Up in 57 minutes. Down in 40 minutes.
Starting Elevation: 12,154 feet (Tincup Pass)
Elevation Gain: 1,258 feet (includes 150 feet lost at the beginning).
Difficulty: Easy
Trail: For the first half (i.e.: from trailhead to the saddle)
Relevant Maps: Cumberland Pass 7½ minute
Chaffee County Number Two
Gunnison County Number Five
Gunnison National Forest
San Isabel National Forest
Views from the summit: N to Taylor Park
NE to Tincup Pass and Emma Burr Mountain
W to Napoleon Pass, Napoleon Mountain and
Fairview Peak

Comment:

Tincup Pass has been a route from the east to the town of Tincup since the 1800s. It was first a burro trail and later a toll road. Continuing improvements have made this road more passable in recent years. This area abounds with history of the early mining of Colorado silver and gold.

Directions to the trailhead:

Drive to Tincup Pass. From the east drive south from the U.S. 24 east and north intersection below Buena Vista on U.S. 285 for 5.7 miles and then turn west onto Chaffee County Road 162. Continue west for 16.2 miles to the historic town of Saint Elmo. Turn right in the center of town, cross a bridge and turn left on Chaffee County Road 267. This road continues up for 6.3 more miles to Tincup Pass which is marked with a sign. Most passenger cars can make the pass from the east.

From the west, Tincup Pass is reached via Cumberland Pass, Taylor Park or Cottonwood Pass via the town of Tincup. It is 6.7 miles from Tincup to Tincup Pass. Four wheel drive will probably be needed for the last half of the western access to the pass from Tincup (i.e. from Mirror Lake). Park at Tincup Pass where ample off-road space can be found. If you must park before the pass, add the extra distance and altitude gain to these directions since they pertain to a hike from the pass.

The Hike:

Drop down about 150 feet to the southwest and keep to the left of the talus. Fitzpatrick Peak is the prominent mountain visible to the southwest. Find a sometimes faint trail and head for the saddle to the right of Fitzpatrick Peak. En route you pass along a shelf leading to a large cairn at the saddle. The trail continues west and down to Napoleon Pass but you leave the trail at the saddle and go directly south up the ridge to a cairn at the top. The best route down is as you ascended. (If you want a side trip to Napoleon Pass and possibly Napoleon Mountain, descend the ridge going north partway to the saddle and then turn west and either continue west on the trail from the saddle or head more directly west to unmarked Napoleon Pass which connects Tincup with the south side of the Cumberland Pass road.)

36

Fitzpatrick Peak from Tincup Pass

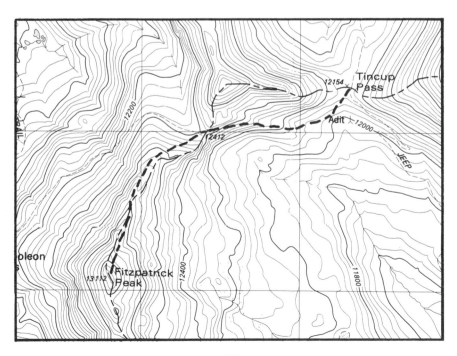

20. Mount Zion 7,059 feet and Lookout Mountain 7,560 feet

Hike Distance: Mount Zion: 0.6 miles each way
Lookout Mountain: 1.3 miles each way
Hiking Time: Mount Zion: Up in 21 minutes. Down in 18 minutes.
Lookout Mountain: Up in 38 minutes. Down in 25 minutes.
Starting Elevation: 6,900 feet (Windy Saddle) for each
Elevation Gain: Mount Zion: 459 feet (includes 150 feet of extra elevation lost each way).
Lookout Mountain: 660 feet
Difficulty: Easy
Trail: All the way to each summit
Relevant Maps: Morrison 7½ minute
Jefferson County Number One

Views from the summits: **From Mount Zion**
N to North Table Mountain
NE to Golden and South Table Mountain
E to Denver
S to Lookout Mountain
SE to Green Mountain
SW to Squaw Mountain
W to Centennial Cone and James Peak

From Lookout Mountain
N to Mount Zion
NE to Golden and North Table Mountain
ENE to South Table Mountain
E to Denver
WNW to Contennial Cone and James Peak
S to Mount Morrison
SE to Green Mountain
SW to Squaw Mountain

Comment:

Mount Zion has a large letter M on its east flank which can be seen for a considerable distance. Lookout Mountain like Mount Zion, is one of several peaks so named in Colorado. Its summit can be reached by a paved road. There are museums, restaurants and homes around the summit mesa. The trails to both summits are part of the Jefferson County Open Space trail system.

Directions to the trailhead:

Drive from U.S. 6 in Golden southwest and up on 19th street, through two pillars for 3.5 miles from U.S. 6 to a parking area and a sign for the Beaver Brook Trail on the west side of the road. Park here.

The Hike:

For Mount Zion proceed due north up the ridge on a rough dirt road from the parking area. A Jefferson County trail sign is present at the beginning. After twelve minutes of steep going you reach the high point of the ridge but this is not designated the Mount Zion summit. Continue north on the ridge and lose about 150 feet before you ascend an unmarked rocky knob which is considered the summit. It will take you about 9 minutes to get here from the high point. You may wish to continue 8 minutes farther north and a bit lower on the ridge to a metal pole in the rock and the end of the faint trail. Return via the same ridge to the trailhead.

A separate hike which can be combined with the Mount Zion ascent is up Lookout Mountain. From the parking area take the Beaver Brook Trail west from the trail sign. After 0.3 miles the Lookout Mountain Trail forks up and south through trees. In 38 minutes from the parking area you reach the summit mesa of Lookout Mountain and Colorow Road. Just across the road is the Jefferson County Conference and Nature Center which has exhibits and two loop trails. The Center building at 7,560 feet is the Lookout Mountain high point. A trail passes along the west side of the Conference and Nature Center and eventually connects with the Apex Trail. The Buffalo Bill Museum is another nearby mountain top point of interest. To descend take the same trail on which you ascended.

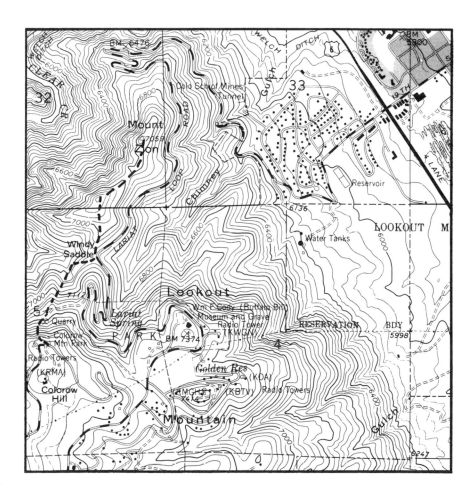

21. Chief Mountain 11,709 feet

Hike Distance: 1.5 miles each way
Hiking Time: Up in 45 minutes. Down in 39 minutes.
Starting Elevation: 10,680 feet
Elevation Gain: 1,129 feet (includes 50 extra feet each way)
Difficulty: Easy (some easy hand work at the top).
Trail: All the way
Relevant Maps: Idaho Springs 7½ minute
Clear Creek County
Arapaho National Forest
Views from the summit: NNW to South Arapaho Peak, Longs Peak, Mount
Meeker and Twin Sisters Peak
NW to James Peak
ENE to Squaw Mountain
S to Bandit Peak
SSW to Rosalie Peak
SE to Pikes Peak
SW to Mount Evans
W to Grays Peak and Torreys Peak

Comment:

This readily accessible peak offers wonderful vistas at and near the top. It forms a mountain family with Squaw Mountain and Papoose Mountain in the middle.

Directions to the trailhead:

Drive west from the town of Bergen Park on Colorado 103 for 13.0 miles (3.8 miles from Squaw Pass). There will be a well graded area off the road on the right (with ski lift machinery just below) and a wooden pole and a trail going initially southeast on the left (south) side of the road. Just above the trailhead on the south side of the road is a cement marker with the number 290 on it. Park off the road in the clear area on the north side of the road.

The Hike:

Proceed southeast by trail on the south side of the road. Enter the trees and cross a dirt road after 0.4 miles. Continue up and southeast. After another 0.3 miles the trail curves south at a cairn. (At this point you are at a saddle with Papoose Mountain, an easy bushwhack up to the northeast.) Continue on the good trail past timberline to finally reach the rocky summit in a clockwise direction. A benchmark and register cylinder lie at the high point. Enjoy the scenery and return by your ascent route.

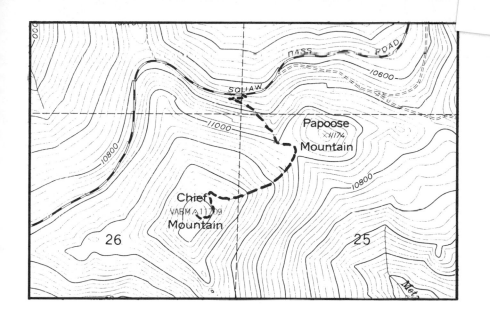

22. Lily Mountain 9,786 feet

Hike Distance: 2.2 miles each way
Hiking Time: Up in 55 minutes. Down in 53 minutes.
Starting Elevation: 8,780 feet
Elevation Gain: 1,336 feet (includes 165 extra feet each way)

Difficulty: Easy
Trail: All the way
Relevant Maps: Longs Peak 7½ minute
                    Larimer County Number Three
                    Roosevelt National Forest
Views from the summit: NNE to Lake Estes
                    NW to the Mummy Range and the YMCA Camp of
                    the Rockies
                    SSW to the Estes Cone, Mount Meeker and Longs
                    Peak
                    SE to Twin Sisters Peaks
                    W to Hallett Peak and Flattop Mountain
Comment:

This hike lies just outside of Rocky Mountain National Park. The vista from
the summit is impressive, especially the view of Longs Peak. Lily Lake lies
to the south and is not encountered on this route nor is any running water.

Directions to the trailhead:

Drive on Colorado 7 either 27.7 miles northwest from Lyons at the junction
with US 36 or 6 miles south from Estes Park at the junction with US 36. The
trail and a sign lie off the west side of the road. Park close to this point off
of the road and be careful due to the fast moving traffic.

The Hike:

Begin north from the trail sign. Pass a trail register and continue northwest for 1.1 miles until the trail curves up and to the left. Avoid faint side trails. The final 50 yards ascend directly south southwest at a faint fork. Follow cairns steeply to the flat, unmarked summit. Some easy hand work may be needed. If you reach a ridge saddle, you have gone too far. (The high point will lie to the northwest.)

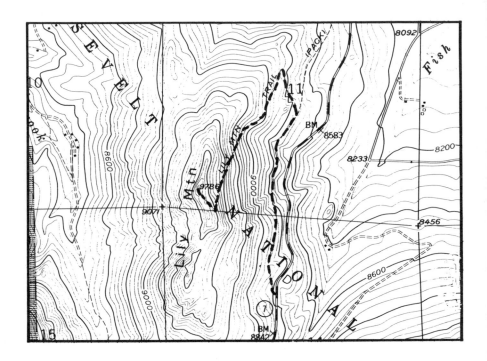

23. Green Mountain 6,855 feet

Hike Distance: 2.25 miles each way
Hiking Time: Up in 60 minutes. Down in 45 minutes.
Starting Elevation: 6,060 feet
Elevation Gain: 895 feet (includes 50 feet extra elevation gain each way)
Difficulty: Easy
Trail: All the way
Relevant Maps: Morrison 7½ minute
                   Jefferson County Number One

Views from the summit: NE to Denver
NW to Lookout Mountain, Longs Peak, Chiefs Head Peak, Pagoda Mountain and Mount Meeker
SW to Mount Morrison, Meridian Hill and Mount Evans
SSE to Pikes Peak and Long Scraggy Peak
W to Chief Mountain
WNW to James Peak
WSW to Squaw Mountain

Comment:

This is the shorter of the two Green Mountains in Jefferson County and the first named foothill as you leave Denver going west. Green Mountain is one of the excellent recreational areas of the City of Lakewood. This hike can be done from March to November.

Directions to trailhead:

The trailhead lies at a parking area on the north side of West Alameda Parkway east of West Utah Avenue. This site is 1.75 miles southwest of Union Boulevard coming from the east on West Alameda Parkway or 0.8 miles east of West Jewell on West Alameda Parkway.

The Hike:

Proceed north northeast and follow the trail as it curves gradually to the northwest and then to the west. When you reach a radio tower building in about 35 minutes, keep left and hike northwest on the summit mesa. Lose a little elevation and near the high point leave the trail and go left over the tundra for about 50 yards to three rock piles at the summit.

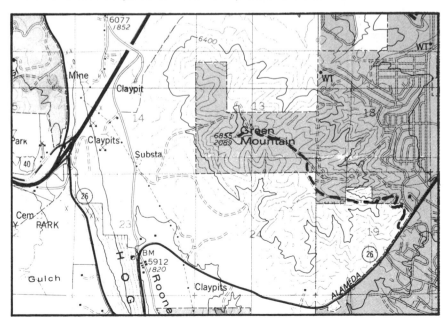

24. Coon Hill 12,757 feet

Hike Distance: 1.3 miles each way
Hiking Time: Up in 66 minutes. Down in 42 minutes.
Starting Elevation: 11,140 feet
Elevation Gain: 1,637 feet (includes 10 extra feet each way)
Difficulty: Easy (but steep)
Trail: Initial 0.3 miles only.
Relevant Maps: Loveland Pass 7½ minute
                      Summit County Number One
                      Grand County Number Four
                      Arapaho National Forest - Dillon Ranger District
Views from the summit: N to Vasquez Peak
                      NNE to Citadel Peak (unofficial name), Hagar
                      Mountain and Pettingell Peak
                      NW to Ute Peak
                      ESE to Torreys Peak and Grays Peak
                      SW to Lake Dillon and the Tenmile Range
                      W to the Gore Range

Comment:

Coon Hill with its southern, rocky subpeak is prominent to the northeast as one approaches the Eisenhower-Edwin C. Johnson Memorial Tunnel from the west. It is the highest named peak in the Williams River Mountain Range. The Eisenhower-Edwin C. Johnson Memorial Tunnel is named after the 34th president of the United States and after a former Governor of Colorado who also served 18 years in the United States Senate. The first bore of the tunnel opened in 1973 and its second bore in 1979. It courses through a flank of Mount Trelease for a length of 8941 feet.

Directions to the trailhead:

Via Interstate 70 drive to the west end of the Eisenhower-Johnson Memorial Tunnel. From the parking area on the north side of the highway drive east on the paved road which passes to the left of an administrative building for 0.2 miles until the road is blocked. Park here on the side of the road.

The Hike:

Begin east on the dirt road and turn left (north) within one hundred feet. Continue 0.2 miles up this road and reach a small cement building between two lanes of the road. Coon Hill will be visible as the high point to the west northwest. Leave the road and proceed west across the creek and up over grassy slopes and some rocks to the saddle on the right side of a rocky subpeak. Then ascend the ridge to the right (north) and reach a register cylinder, a cairn and a benchmark at the summit. On your descent to the east avoid the steep rocky areas and stay on tundra wherever possible.

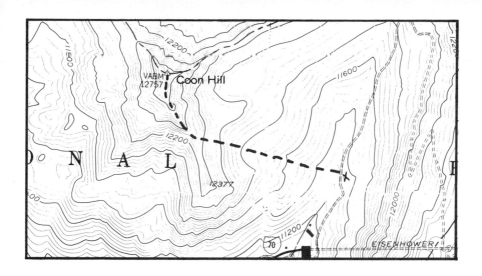

25. Diamond Peaks 11,852 feet (Highest point)

Hike Distance: 1.4 miles on the ascent and 1.1 miles for the descent
                    (loop)
Hiking Time: Up in 66 minutes. Down in 33 minutes.
Starting Elevation: 10,276 feet (Cameron Pass)
Elevation Gain: 1,576 feet
Difficulty: Easy
Trail: From trailhead up into the basin (First half).
Relevant Maps: Clark Peak 7½ minute
                    Larimer County Number Three
                    Roosevelt National Forest
Views from the summit: N to Cameron Peak
                    NE to Joe Wright Reservoir
                    NNW to Clark Peak
                    E to Iron Mountain
                    ESE to Longs Peak
                    SSE to the Nokhu Crags and Mount Richthofen

Comment:

This group of peaks are located about 30 miles south of the Wyoming state line and are to be distinguished from Diamond Peak which lies to the northeast, is much closer to Wyoming, also in Larimer County and is 8,668 feet high. The details given describe the route to the highest of these peaks. Cameron Pass was discovered by General R.A. Cameron who also founded the city of Fort Collins.

Directions to the trailhead:

Drive on Colorado 14 to Cameron Pass. From the east the pass is 59.3 miles from the edge of Fort Collins where U.S. 287 and Colorado 14 intersect.

45

From the west, Cameron Pass is about 33.5 miles east of Walden on Colorado 14. Park in the designated area by a picnic ground on the west side of the pass.

The Hike:

Head WSW from your car up into the trees and find the trail. You will reach a creek which you should keep on your right. Stay on the trail and ascend alongside the creek. The trail fades as you reach an open basin at the foot of the peaks. The highest peak will be visible to the northwest. It has a distinct hump near its summit and is your target. Proceed to the ridge on the south side of the summit and then ascend over tundra to the top which is marked by an U.S.G.S. marker, a cairn, a metal pole and several pieces of wood and wire. To descend hike directly down (southeast) from the summit to the trail you left at the basin.

The Nokhu Crags and Mount Richthofen from the Diamond Peaks

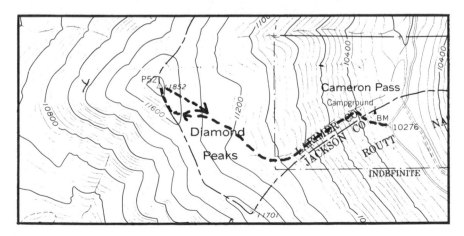

26. Mount Sniktau 13,234 feet

Hike Distance: 1.5 miles each way
Hiking Time: Up in 71 minutes. Down in 52 minutes.
Starting Elevation: 11,990 feet (Loveland Pass)
Elevation Gain: 1,244 feet
Difficulty: Easy
Trail: All the way
Relevant Maps: Loveland Pass 7½ minute
                    Grays Peak 7½ minute
                    Clear Creek County
                    Arapaho National Forest
Views from the summit: N to Woods Mountain
                    NE to Mount Parnassus and Bard Peak
                    NW to Mount Trelease and Hagar Mountain
                    S to Grizzly Peak
                    SE to Torreys Peak

Comment:

Sniktau was a pen name used by E.H.N. Patterson, a Clear Creek County journalist of the mid 1800s. From Virginia, he edited the Georgetown Courier and was associated with the writer, Edgar Allen Poe.

This hike has a high, easily accessible starting point, a very unambiguous route and is totally above timberline. Mount Sniktau is seen prominently from I-70 as one drives west from Silver Plume.

Directions to the trailhead:

Drive to Loveland Pass either from the north via I-70 and U.S. 6 or from the south via U.S.6 from Lake Dillon and the Keystone area. Park in the paved area near the Loveland Pass sign.

The Hike:

Take the clear trail going northeast up the ridge. The trail passes four cairn marked knobs en route to the fifth and highest cairn on the Mount Sniktau summit. The descent route is identical.

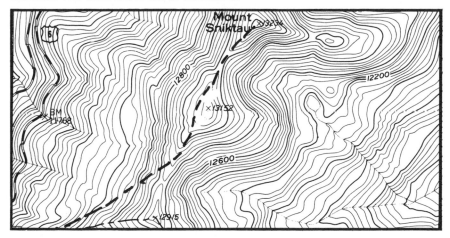

27. West White Pine Mountain 10,305 feet

Hike Distance: 2.6 miles each way
Hiking Time: Up in 76 minutes. Down in 54 minutes.
Starting Elevation: 8,288 feet
Elevation Gain: 2,017 feet
Difficulty: Easy
Trail: All the way on an old mining road
Relevant Maps: Crystal Mountain 7½ minute
                    Larimer County Number Four
                    Roosevelt National Forest
Views from the summit: E to East White Pine Mountain
                       S to Longs Peak, North Signal Mountain and
                       Lookout Mountain
                       SW to the Mummy Range

Comment:

This hike provides an opportunity to experience the lovely Buckhorn Valley. Buckhorn Creek flows by Masonville into the Big Thompson River west of Loveland. Masonville was named after James R. Mason who was born in Kentucky in 1849 and overcame great poverty to become a successful farmer and cattle rancher in the area.

Directions to the trailhead:

Drive 6.7 miles west on U.S. 34 from its intersection with U.S. 287 in Loveland. Turn right (north) and continue 5.4 more miles to Masonville where the road continues as a T. Take the left turn. After 3.7 miles from Masonville, the road becomes unpaved. Drive 3.5 miles more to a fork. Take the left fork for 11.9 more miles along Buckhorn Creek to the Buckhorn Ranger Station which will be on your left. (The total distance from the intersection in Loveland to the Buckhorn Ranger Station is 31.2 miles.) Just past the Ranger Station on your right is Road 100 going north. When open, this road leads to the summit of West White Pine Mountain but 4 wheel drive is required. Park about 0.2 miles north of the Ranger Station just off Road 100 near the site of the road barrier.

Another route to the trailhead is from Fort Collins via Rist Canyon to Stove Prairie. Drive south from Stove Prairie 3.8 miles and then make a sharp right turn at an intersection and proceed 11.9 miles to the Buckhorn Ranger Station. Regular cars should be able to reach the trailhead either from Loveland or Fort Collins.

The Hike:

Follow the road up and north as it passes through many aspen trees and a meadow. After 1.8 miles you reach a saddle between West and East White Pine Mountains. An U.S.G.S. marker lies just north of the road. Follow the road as it turns up and west from the saddle. In 0.8 miles from the saddle the road brings you to the top of West White Pine Mountain which is covered by ruins of an old lookout structure. Four cement pillars and a makeshift bench mark the summit. Trees block some of the views but to the southwest and west it is open. Follow the road back to your car. (If you want to reach the lower East White Pine summit as well, bushwhack up and east from the saddle. This will require about 22 minutes up and 16 minutes back

48

down to the saddle and 608 feet of extra elevation gain. The east summit lies amid some rock formations which are easily negotiated. Do not descend southwest from the summit to save time lest you pass south of a 9130 foot subpeak and miss Road 100 totally.)

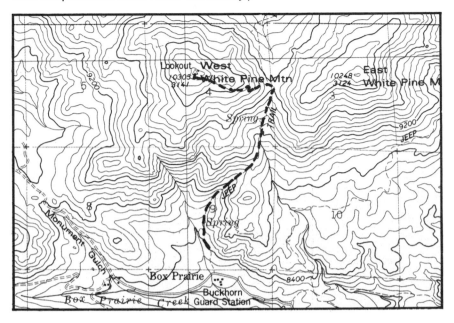

28. Geneva Mountain 12,335 feet

Hike Distance:	3.5 miles each way
Hiking Time:	Up in 88 minutes. Down in 86 minutes.
Starting Elevation:	11,669 feet
Elevation Gain:	822 feet (includes 78 feet extra each way)
Difficulty:	Easy
Trail:	First half
Relevant Maps:	Mount Evans 7½ minute
	Clear Creek County
	Park County Number Two
	Pike National Forest
Views from the summit:	NNE to Mount Bierstadt, Mount Evans and Epaulet Mountain
	NW to Mount Wilcox and Otter Mountain
	E to Bandit Peak
	SSE to North Twin Cone Peak
	SE to Kataka Mountain and Mount Logan
	SW to South Park
	WNW to Square Top Mountain

Comment:

This Geneva Mountain is not to be confused with Geneva Peak which is just north of Webster Pass farther southwest in Park County. Guanella Pass was named after Byron Guanella, a Clear Creek County Commissioner who

49

promoted work on the pass. This hike is all above timberline and therefore affords extensive vistas over its entire length.

Directions to the trailhead:

Drive to Guanella Pass either north from Grant at U.S. 285 or south from Georgetown off of Interstate 70. Park in the designated area by a sign on the east side of the road at the pass. Regular cars can traverse Guanella Pass from either the north or south.

The Hike:

Begin south southeast on the trail from the Guanella Pass parking area. In 5 minutes take the left fork and continue on Trail 603. Within ten more minutes you will see Geneva Mountain and two subpeaks to its right. Continue on an old road for about 30 minutes from the trailhead and then leave the road and ascend southeast mostly over tundra. Skirt the first subpeak to the left (east) and cross directly over the second subpeak to reach the top of Geneva Mountain with a small rock pile and a register jar.

Geneva Mountain from the northwest

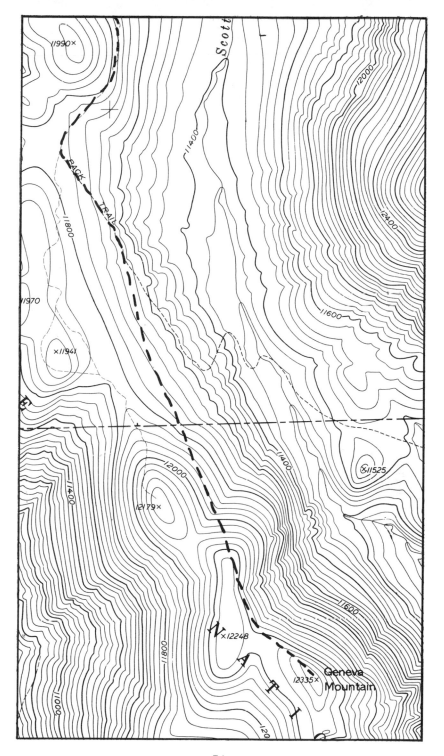

29. Glacier Peak 12,853 feet

Hike Distance: 2.9 miles each way
Hiking Time: Up in 72 minutes. Down in 63 minutes.
Starting Elevation: 11,585 feet (Georgia Pass)
Elevation Gain: 1,368 feet (includes 50 feet of extra elevation gain each way).
Difficulty: Easy
Trail: All the way to just below the summit
Relevant Maps: Boreas Pass 7½ Minute
                     Park County Number One
                     Pike National Forest
Views from the summit: N to Grays Peak and Torreys Peak
                     NE to Whale Peak
                     NW to Lake Dillon
                     ESE to North Twin Cone Peak
                     SE to South Park
                     SW to Mount Guyot

Comment:

The town of Jefferson was once a gold mining camp and then later a railroad shipping station. The railroad tracks were removed in the 1930s. The town, Jefferson Lake, Jefferson Creek and Jefferson Hill were all named to honor President Thomas Jefferson.

Directions to the trailhead:

At Jefferson in South Park drive northwest from US 285 on the National Forest access road for 11.7 miles to Georgia Pass and park off road. Regular cars can reach the pass from Jefferson but not from Colorado 9 north of Breckenridge. En route to Georgia Pass from US 285 at Jefferson keep straight at mile 1.9, go right at mile 2.8 and left at mile 5.2. Go straight at mile 5.8, right at mile 6.4 and right again at mile 6.8. The last two forks are also to the right at mile 11.4 and at mile 11.5 before you reach the pass with Mount Guyot on the left.

The Hike:

Proceed northeast on the rough road to Glacier Ridge. Cross an intersection with the Colorado Trail and continue to ascend above timberline along the Continental Divide to reach a four-way trail intersection after 0.7 miles. Continue up more steeply and cross two false summits. Finally leave the dirt road and ascend right to a rock pile and a benchmark at the top of Glacier Peak. (The ridge continues northeast to the top of Whale Peak in 1.5 miles.) Return as you ascended.

Route to Glacier Peak

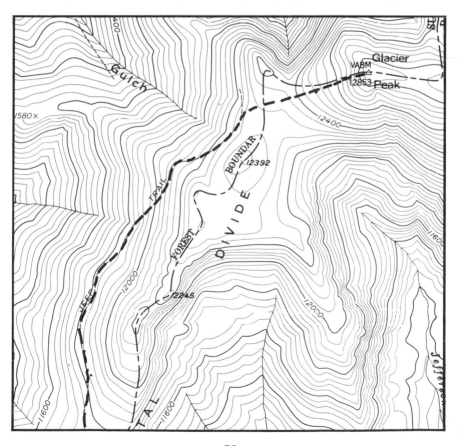

30. Mount Volz 12,489 feet

Hike Distance: 1.75 miles each way
Hiking Time: Up in 79 minutes. Down in 58 minutes.
Starting Elevation: 10,900 feet (Georgia Pass)
Elevation Gain: 1,689 feet
Difficulty: Easy
Trail: First half
Relevant Maps: Boreas Pass 7½ minute
 Park County Number One
 Pike National Forest
Views from the summit: N to Grays Peak and Torreys Peak
 NE to South Park
 NNW to Mount Guyot
 NW to Bald Mountain and Boreas Mountain
 SSW to Little Baldy Mountain
 SW to Mount Silverheels
 W to Pacific Peak

Comment:

Access to this peak from the east is blocked by the Volz Ranch. To reach this summit follow the directions carefully since there are several unnamed high points in the area. Mount Volz can be seen from the trailhead to the ENE and throughout the hike.

Directions to the trailhead:

Drive north from U.S. 285 on the Boreas Pass Road through Como for a total of 8.2 miles (from U.S. 285) or south from Boreas Pass for 3.1 miles to a bend in the road, a creek crossing and a blocked-off side road leading up and to the east. Park off the road near this side road. Regular cars can usually negotiate the entire Boreas Pass Road.

The Hike:

Go east on the old road which soon curves south and then crosses the creek and rises to the east and timberline. As the road ends, continue due north over talus to a saddle with Mount Volz to your left and a small rocky knob to your right. Proceed west up the talus ridge to a large summit cairn, a rock shelter and an U.S.G.S. marker within a circle of rocks. Return as you ascended.

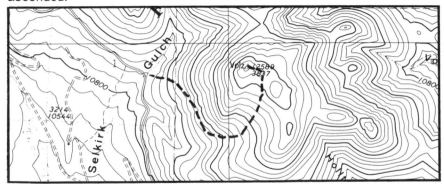

31. Round Hill 11,243 feet

Hike Distance: 3.2 miles each way
Hiking Time: Up in 80 minutes. Down in 70 minutes.
Starting Elevation: 10,080 feet
Elevation Gain: 1,163 feet
Difficulty: Easy
Trail: All the way until 300 feet from the top.
Relevant Maps: Fairplay West 7½ minute
    Park County Number One
    Pike National Forest
Views from the summit: N to Mount Silverheels
    NW to Horseshoe Mountain, Mount Sherman and
    Sheep Mountain
    W to Weston Peak and Ptarmigan Peak

Comment:

Despite the name, Breakneck Pass can easily be reached by four wheel drive. Fairplay was originally called South Park City and once had a population as high as 8000. It was renamed as a retort to Tarryall which locals called "Graball." Como was originally the Stubbs Ranch and was named after Lake Como by the many Italian workers who lived there.

Directions to the trailhead:

Either drive north from the cutoff to Como on U.S. 285 for 4.75 miles or drive south from the Colorado 9 West intersection with U.S. 285 at Fairplay for 4.75 miles. Coming from either direction, turn west onto Park County Road Number 5 which is the more northerly route to Weston Pass from the east. After 1.7 miles on this road, a side road leads to the right at a sign "Breakneck Pass Road—Private Property next 1.5 miles. Stay on Main Road." Follow this road which is passable to regular cars for at least 1.65 miles to a sign stating that you are entering the Pike National Forest. Park off the road at this point.

The Hike:

Proceed on the mining road designated Number 175 as it leads west and then southwest in 1.8 miles to Breakneck Pass. At the pass, which is well forested, take a mining road which leads southeast (left) off the main road. Follow this road as it gradually ascends to just east of the summit. Leave the road and hike about 100 yards west to the unmarked, tree-covered summit. Return by the same route. (N.B. About 50 yards west of Breakneck Pass there is a four way intersection. Road 175 goes east and west with the western road passing into Sheep Park. Road 426 goes north to dead-end along Sheep Ridge and south to join the Weston Pass Road.)

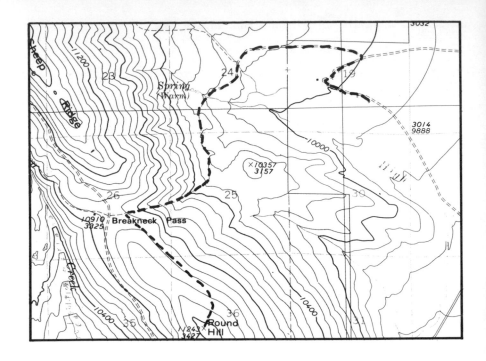

32. Kingston Peak 12,147 feet

Hike Distance: 1.9 miles each way
Hiking Time: Up in 82 minutes. Down in 58 minutes.
Starting Elevation: 10,470 feet
Elevation Gain: 1,677 feet
Difficulty: Easy
Trail: Only to St. Marys Lake
Relevant Maps: Empire 7½ minute
Clear Creek County
Arapaho National Forest
Views from the summit: NNW to Mount Neva and South Arapaho Peak
SE to Squaw Mountain, Papoose Mountain and Chief Mountain
SSW to Square Top Mountain, Grays Peak and Torreys Peak
SSE to Mount Evans
SW to Mount Bancroft and Parry Peak
W to James Peak

Comment:

Kingston Peak forms part of the boundary between the Roosevelt and Arapaho National Forests and between Gilpin and Clear Creek Counties. The best time for this hike is late August or early September when St. Marys Glacier is most easily traversed or bypassed.

Directions to the trailhead:

From I-70 two miles west of Idaho Springs take exit 238 and drive north on Fall River Road for 9.7 miles to a right turning curve of the paved road. Turn left at this curve and drive north northwest on the dirt road with Silver Lake on your right (east) for 0.2 miles to a four-way intersection and park off the road. Regular cars can come this far.

The Hike:

Proceed south up an old mining road at the foot of Fox Mountain for about 10 minutes to a bend in the road toward the north. Follow a trail which passes to the west from the road on the north side of the creek. In another 7 minutes this trail will bring you to the east side of Saint Marys Lake. Continue on the trail past the north end of the lake to the area of Saint Marys Glacier where the trail ends. Hike west and up either around or through the icefield for 0.75 miles and then turn north for another 0.6 miles over tundra to a summit cairn with two poles. Descend via your ascent route.

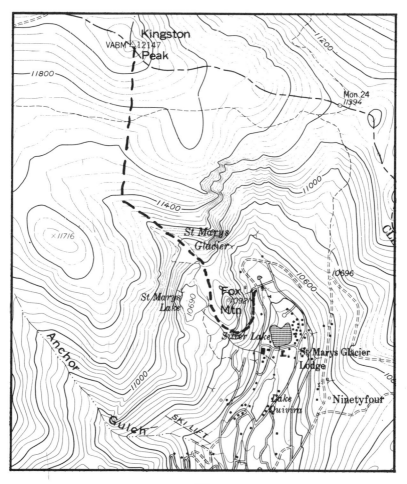

33. Mount Epworth 11,843 feet

Hike Distance: 3.25 miles each way
Hiking Time: Up in 83 minutes. Down in 72 minutes.
Starting Elevation: 11,080 feet
Elevation Gain: 1,263 feet (includes 250 feet of extra elevation gain each way).
Difficulty: Easy (some easy hand work over talus near the top).
Trail: Initial 90%
Relevant Maps: East Portal 7½ minute
                   Grand County Number Four
                   Arapaho National Forest
Views from the summit: NNE to Rollins Pass
                   NNW to Corona Lake
                   S to Parry Peak
                   SE to James Peak
                   SSW to the Winter Park Ski Area
                   SW to St. Louis Peak, Byers Peak and Bottle Peak
                   W to Fraser

Comment:

John Quincy Adams Rollins built a toll road over what once was called Boulder Pass, then Rollins Pass and later, Corona Pass. A railroad also operated over this route until 1937. Epworth is the English village where John and Charles Wesley were born. The Epworth League, a national Methodist organization, named this mountain on July 8, 1905.

Directions to the trailhead:

Drive on U.S. 40 either 11.8 miles north from Berthoud Pass or 1.75 miles south from Vasquez Road in Winter Park. Turn northwest onto the Rollins Pass or Corona Pass road. Follow the road for a total of 11.0 miles to an abandoned railroad trestle on your left at what is known as Riflesight Notch. Regular cars can make it this far if there is no obstructing snow. Park here off the road. En route to this trailhead on the Corona Pass Road, keep right at 3.7 miles, continue straight (southeast) at a 5 way intersection at mile 3.8, keep right on the main road at mile 4.55, keep southeast on the main road at a four way intersection at mile 6.6, keep right at mile 8.6 and again at mile 8.85. In optimal conditions regular vehicles may be able to reach Corona Pass and shorten this hike considerably.

The Hike:

Continue on foot up the road as it winds east and north for 2.5 miles to a point 5 minutes past a sign with the number 17 on your left. Two lakes and Mount Epworth will be to the west (on your left). Near the level of the more northerly Pumphouse Lake an old mining road leaves the main road and descends to the north (left). After about four minutes on this road, take a left fork and soon leave this road and pass to the northwest of the lake and ascend the north ridge of Mount Epworth. Proceed upward and south over tundra and then talus to a modest cairn at the summit. Descend by your ascent route since the loop descent to the southwest from the top loses too much altitude and distance.

Mount Epworth from road south of Rollins Pass

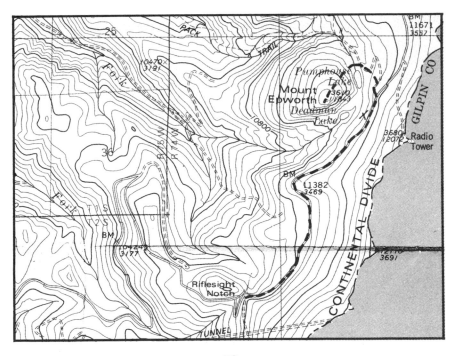

34. Tremont Mountain 10,388 feet

Hike Distance: 1.0 miles each way
Hiking Time: Up in 90 minutes. Down in 60 minutes.
Starting Elevation: 8,860 feet
Elevation Gain: 1,528 feet
Difficulty: Easy (but quite steep with occasional easy hand work
                   around the summit ridge.)
Trail: Initial 25% (the Coyote Trail in Golden Gate Canyon
                   State Park).
Relevant Maps: Black Hawk 7½ minute
                   Gilpin County
                   Golden Gate Canyon State Park
Views from the summit: NNE to Starr Peak (Thorodin Mountain)
                   NNW to Longs Peak
                   NW to Mount Audubon
                   E to Denver
                   SW to Mount Evans
                   SSW to Squaw Mountain

Comment:

Tremont Mountain is the highest point in Golden Gate Canyon State Park. This park is well maintained and contains nearly 60 miles of clearly marked hiking trails.

Directions to the trailhead:

Drive to Golden Gate Canyon State Park either going west from Washington Street in Golden on the Golden Gate Canyon Road (Jefferson County Road 70 which becomes Colorado Road 46) for 14.1 miles, or north on Colorado 119 and then east on Colorado 46. After entering the park, proceed via the Mountain Base Road to the Coyote Trailhead at Bootleg Bottom. Park here.

The Hike:

Begin by going east and up on the Coyote Trail for about one quarter mile to a sharp turn of the trail to the southeast at about 9400 feet. Leave the trail at this point and head northeast and up to the western (left) side of Tremont Mountain. Near the top you will gain a ridge which leads southeast to the rocky summit. A hole drilled into the rock and an upright piece of wood are the only markers. The best route down is as you came up.

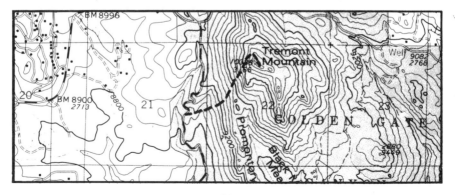

60

35. Mount Sheridan 13,748 feet

Hike Distance: 1.0 miles each way
Hiking Time: Up in 90 minutes. Down in 60 minutes.
Starting Elevation: 12,200 feet
Elevation Gain: 1,548 feet
Difficulty: Easy
Trail: From trailhead part-way to the ridge and then from the ridge to the summit.
Relevant Maps: Mount Sherman 7½ minute
Fairplay West 7½ minute
Park County Number One
Lake County
Pike National Forest
Views from the summit: NE to Mount Sherman and Gemini Peak
S to Peerless Mountain and Horseshoe Mountain
SW and W to the Collegiate Peaks
SW to Twin Lakes

Comment:

This area is rich in mining history. The Last Chance Mine was located on the side of Mount Sheridan. Another large producer was the Hilltop Mine, located at the saddle between Mount Sheridan and Mount Sherman. Many of the miners lived in the nearby towns of Leavick and Horseshoe which you pass in your car en route to the trailhead. The Denver and South Park Railroad once reached Leavick whose population approximated 200 before the turn of the century.

Directions to the trailhead:

From the junction of Colorado 9 and U.S. 285 in Fairplay, drive south on U.S. 285 for 1.25 miles. Then turn west (right) and follow Park County 18 (also known as the Fourmile Creek Road) for 12.3 miles to two metal posts on each side of the road. (Keep right at the fork near the Leavick site.) Regular cars can drive to this point or close to it. Park here.

The Hike:

Proceed west and up the road to the old Dauntless Mine and then leave the road and hike up and southwest to the saddle between Peerless Mountain to the south and Mount Sheridan to the north. A faint trail goes up the ridge to a small cairn and a makeshift register atop Mount Sheridan. (If you wish to hike up Peerless Mountain to the south, it will add 0.4 miles each way and 208 feet of elevation gain. Mount Sherman is accessible via the ridge to the north.) Descend as you came up by way of the abandoned Dauntless Mine.

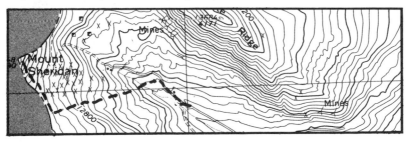

36. Revenue Mountain 12,889 feet

Hike Distance: 1.9 miles each way
Hiking Time: Up in 85 minutes. Down in 70 minutes.
Starting Elevation: 10,850 feet
Elevation Gain: 2,039 feet
Difficulty: Easy
Trail: Up to near timberline in Cinnamon Gulch
Relevant Maps: Montezuma 7½ minute
                    Summit County Number Two
                    Arapaho National Forest
Views from the summit: N to Grays Peak
                    NE to Decatur Mountain and Argentine Peak
                    NW to Brittle Silver Mountain
                    E to Square Top Mountain
                    S to Landslide Peak
                    SW to Santa Fe Peak and Sullivan Mountain
                    W to Silver Mountain

Comment:

Revenue Mountain lies on the boundary between Summit and Clear Creek Counties and is readily accessible also from the southeast via the southern part of the Guanella Pass Road. Peru Gulch was the site of extensive mining in the late eighteen hundreds. This hike should be attempted late in the season when Peru Creek will be lower and more easily crossed.

Directions to the trailhead:

Drive via I-70 and U.S. 6 to the Keystone Ski Area which lies east of Lake Dillon. Turn south off of U.S. 6 on the Montezuma Road. In fifty yards, take the first left turn. Drive east up this road for 4.8 miles from U.S. 6 to the Peru Creek Road which begins on the left at a curve in the road. Drive northeast up Peru Creek for 3.8 miles and turn right off the main road onto an unmarked road. This is the road up Cinnamon Gulch. Park here before Peru Creek is crossed. (With four-wheel drive you can travel 0.85 miles up into the basin for a higher starting point. The hike information given will be based on a start from Peru Creek.)

The Hike:

Go south, cross Peru Creek and stay on the mining road which rises into Cinnamon Gulch. Several side roads lead to old mining operations. At the first three forks go left, right and right as you head toward the basin. In a little less than a mile you arrive at a large, open area and a road fork. Take the right fork and continue south as you ascend further into the basin. Revenue Mountain will be visible to the southeast. Just below timberline leave the road and go directly south and up over easy tundra to the saddle between Silver Mountain on the right and Revenue Mountain on the left. An old mining cabin lies below the Revenue Mountain summit. Follow the ridge then eastward to the top which has a cairn and a small register jar. Decatur Mountain to the northeast, Silver Mountain to the west and Brittle Silver Mountain to the northwest are all accessible by easy ridge walks from Revenue Mountain. Descend as you came up unless you wish to walk the ridge to some of these other nearby peaks.

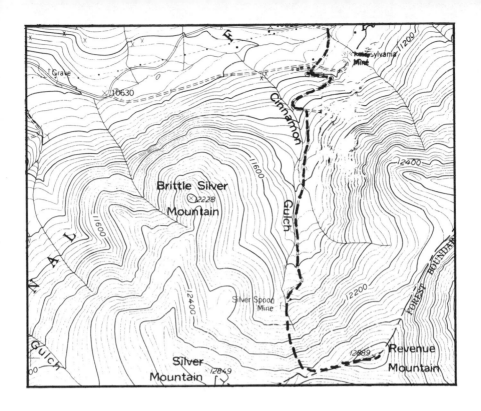

37. Woods Mountain 12,940 feet

Hike Distance: 2.55 miles each way
Hiking Time: Up in 88 minutes. Down in 70 minutes.
Starting Elevation: 10,800 feet
Elevation Gain: 2,190 feet (includes 25 feet of extra elevation gain each
                    way).
Difficulty: Easy
Trail: Initial 60%
Relevant Maps: Berthoud Pass 7½ minute
                    Grays Peak 7½ minute
                    Clear Creek County
                    Arapaho National Forest
Views from the summit: N to Red Mountain and Urad Lake
                    NNW to Vasquez Peak
                    NE to Engelmann Peak
                    ESE to Mount Parnassus
                    S to Mount Guyot and Bald Mountain
                    SE to Torreys Peak, Grizzly Peak and Mount Sniktau
                    SW to Hagar Mountain
                    W to Pettingell Peak
                    WSW to Mount Bethel

Comment:

From Woods Mountain one can ascend the ridge to the east southeast and easily reach Mount Parnassus and Bard Peak or descend southwest to a saddle and then continue west up the ridge to reach Pettingell Peak.

Directions to the trailhead:

Drive west from U.S. 40 on the Henderson Mine cutoff road 5.9 miles south of Berthoud Pass or 7.4 miles west of Empire. In 0.4 miles turn left toward Urad Lake. You will drive a total of 3.65 miles southwest from U.S. 40 to a creek crossing at the inlet to Urad Lake. Park here. En route to this point, go straight at 1.7 miles, keep right at 2.7 miles, keep left at 2.8 miles and continue straight at 3.1 miles and stay above Urad Lake.

The Hike:

Proceed on the road as it curves north and then returns to its southwesterly route into the gulch along Woods Creek. After 0.5 miles take the right fork and keep the creek on your left. In 0.6 miles further follow the road as it crosses the creek and soon ends just below timberline. Continue south southwest toward the head of the valley. Turn south and gain the ridge over tundra wherever the route appears easiest. At the ridge follow a faint trail which goes east over a false summit to the nondescript, flat, unmarked top of Woods Mountain. To return either retrace your ascent route or descend to the north northwest over steep tundra to Woods Creek and the road back to your vehicle.

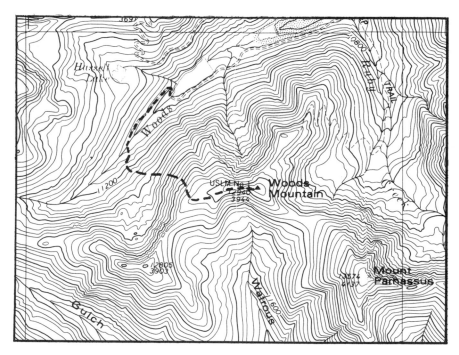

38. Little Baldy Mountain 12,142 feet

Hike Distance:	2.0 miles each way
Hiking Time:	Up in 88 minutes. Down in 76 minutes.
Starting Elevation:	10,240 feet
Elevation Gain:	2,002 feet (includes 50 feet of extra elevation gain each way).
Difficulty:	Moderate
Trail:	Initial 25%
Relevant Maps:	Como 7½ minute
	Park County Number One
	Pike National Forest
Views from the summit:	N to Bald Mountain, Boreas Mountain and Mount Guyot
	NE to Mount Volz and Mount Logan
	SE to East and West Buffalo Peaks
	SSE to Pikes Peak
	W to Mount Silverheels
	WSW to Palmer Peak

Comment:

This is the prominent peak at the southwest end of the Boreas Pass Road. Some private homes exist in the area but no prohibiting signs are to be seen throughout this route.

Directions to the trailhead:

Drive west from U.S. 285 on the Boreas Pass Road through Como for 3.4 miles and arrive at a fork. The right fork goes to Boreas Pass. Take the left fork west and then northwest for 0.8 miles and avoid another right fork. Take a faint road going off to the left (southwest) for 0.06 miles and park at a barrier blocking further vehicular traffic.

The Hike:

Continue on the road, pass under the chain preventing vehicular access and cross Tarryall Creek on an earthen bridge. Follow the road as it curves to the left (southeast). In about 8 minutes from the trailhead, take a right fork and continue southeast. The road soon ends at two private cabins. Avoiding any private property, hike due south and lose 50 feet of elevation as you descend toward South Tarryall Creek. Keep to the right of the creek and 3 abandoned cabins. Little Baldy Mountain may now be visible directly south. Enter the woods following an abandoned road which heads west. When the road becomes obscure, continue to bushwhack up and south through the relatively sparse forest. You eventually reach a talus slope followed by some more trees and then more talus. Above timberline a cairn on top of a false summit marks the route. The high point lies at the south end of a mesa and is marked by a rock cairn with an embedded pole. An animal skull was on the pole on the day I was there. Retrace your ascent route for the return.

Little Baldy Mountain from South Tarryall Creek

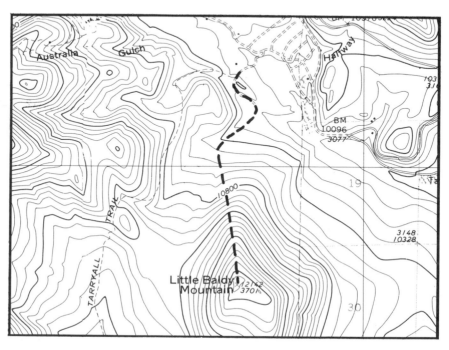

39. Kelso Mountain 13,164 feet

Hike Distance:	2.75 miles on the ascent. 1.5 miles on the descent (loop).
Hiking Time:	Up in 93 minutes. Down in 54 minutes.
Starting Elevation:	11,230 feet
Elevation Gain:	1,934 feet
Difficulty:	Moderate
Trail:	Initial 1.9 miles on the ascent. Final one mile on the descent.
Relevant Maps:	Grays Peak 7½ minute
	Clear Creek County
	Arapaho National Forest
Views from the summit:	N to Longs Peak and Mount Meeker
	NNE to Silver Plume Mountain, Sherman Mountain and Republican Mountain
	NE to Ganley Mountain
	NNW to Woods Mountain, Mount Parnassus and Bard Peak
	ESE to Gray Wolf Mountain, Mount Spalding and Mount Evans
	S to Grays Peak
	SSW to Torreys Peak
	SE to Mount McClellan and Mount Edwards
	SW to Grizzly Peak
	W to Baker Mountain, Mount Sniktau, Hagar Mountain , Mount Bethel and Pettingell Peak

Comment:

This mountain is named after William Fletcher Kelso, a local prospector in the mining era. The mountain was to be pierced by a railroad tunnel but this was never completed.

Directions to the trailhead:

Drive south from the Bakerville Exit (Number 221) of Interstate 70 for 3.4 miles to the trailhead. The road Is blocked just before the Stevens Mine further south. En route to the parking area near the trailhead, take left forks at mile 1.35 and at mile 2.3. A regular car can make it up this steep, rough road to the trailhead area.

The Hike:

Cross the creek and quickly access the old mining road going southwest up Stevens Gulch. This road is closed to vehicles. In almost two miles the road has become a trail and crosses the creek amid two cairns. Leave the trail (which continues up to Grays Peak) at this point and ascend north northeast over steep tundra to gain the ridge. At the ridge continue north to the summit cairn. The best descent route is over very steep tundra to the east to regain the trail which leads back to the trailhead.

Grays Peak and Torreys Peak from Kelso Mountain

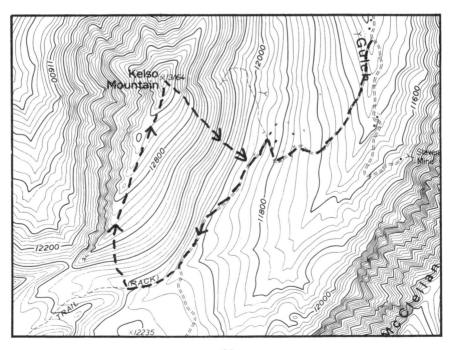

40. Bottle Peak 11,584 feet

Hike Distance:	1.75 miles each way
Hiking Time:	Up in 57 minutes. Down in 35 minutes.
Starting Elevation:	10,440 feet
Elevation Gain:	1,194 feet (includes 25 feet of extra elevation gain each way).
Difficulty:	Easy
Trail:	All the way
Relevant Maps:	Bottle Pass 7½ minute
	Grand County Number Four
	Arapaho National Forest
Views from the summit:	NE to Fraser
	S to Byers Peak
	SSW to Bills Peak
	SE to Vasquez Peak
	WNW to Ptarmigan Peak

Comment:

Grand County is named after its Grand Lake and the Grand River which was renamed the Colorado River.

The town of Fraser and the Fraser River which runs through it were named for Reuben Frazier, an early settler of the area. The respelling occured after a post office was begun in the town. Fraser calls itself "the icebox of the nation" due to the frequently recorded low temperatures there.

Directions to the trailhead:

From U.S. 40 at Fraser (northwest of Winter Park and southeast of Granby), drive west on Eisenhower Drive at a sign directing you to Town Park. Drive past the library on your left, cross the railroad tracks and make an immediate left turn onto Leonard Lane. This road runs parallel to the train tracks and curves right to become Mills Avenue and forest road 160. Continue on this good, main, dirt road as it leads southwest up the valley. From U.S. 40, you will take the following forks: right at mile 2.8, left at mile 4.7, straight at a 4-way intersection at mile 4.8, right at mile 6.5, right at mile 7.2 (at the Byers Creek Campground sign), right at mile 7.5, (follow the sign to Bottle Pass trail), right at mile 9.5, left at mile 9.6, right at mile 9.9, right at mile 10.5, left at mile 10.7 and reach the trail sign to Bottle Pass on the right at mile 12.0. Park off the road here. Regular cars can reach this point and road end 0.4 miles further.

The Hike:

Begin west up the trail. After some switchbacks you will reach a ridge and tundra just below timberline after 0.8 miles. Then turn right and follow a series of cairns north northwest up to the top of Bottle Peak. A pole in a rock pile marks this point. (Bottle Pass is a few hundred yards to the west with Ptarmigan Peak not far beyond.) Return as you ascended.

Byers Peak and Bills Peak from Bottle Pass

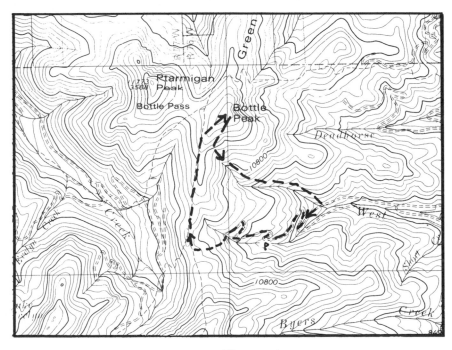

41. Griffith Mountain 11,558 feet

Hike Distance: 2.5 miles each way
Hiking Time: Up in 100 minutes. Down in 60 minutes.
Starting Elevation: 9,100 feet
Elevation Gain: 2,568 feet (includes 50 feet of extra elevation gain each way).
Difficulty: Moderate
Trail: Initial 50%
Relevant Maps: Georgetown 7½ minute
                  Clear Creek County
                  Arapaho National Forest
Views from the summit: S to Sugarloaf Peak
                  SE to Gray Wolf Mountain and Mount Spalding
                  SW to Square Top Mountain

Comment:

This mountain is named after two early Clear Creek miners, the Griffith brothers, David and George. Georgetown was named after the later.

This hike involves one mile of bushwhacking to and from the top. The views from the summit are best to the south, southeast and southwest with many trees obscuring vistas in the other directions.

Directions to the trailhead:

Drive southwest from I-70 at the town of Idaho Springs on Colorado 103 for 6.7 miles. At a sharp bend in the road, a dirt road leads southwest up West Chicago Creek. Drive up this road for 1.1 miles to an area on the right (north) just before a group of houses and a creek flowing to the southeast and under the road. Being careful to avoid private property, park off the road in this general area.

The Hike:

Continue on foot up the public road about 200 yards southwest of the creek crossing. Just past the houses on your right leave the road and ascend steeply northwest and within one hundred feet gain an abandoned mining road passing to the west. Take this road and continue to ascend to the west. Stay on the road which crosses a ridge and descends a bit before resuming its upward WNW direction. Eventually an old cabin is reached to the left of the road in a clearing. Leave the road at this point and enter a relatively sparse area of forest on your right and ascend northwest over many decaying tree fragments all the way to the top. The summit lies on a small natural rock formation and has no identifying markers. Return by the same route, bushwhacking southeast about a mile until you reach the trail.

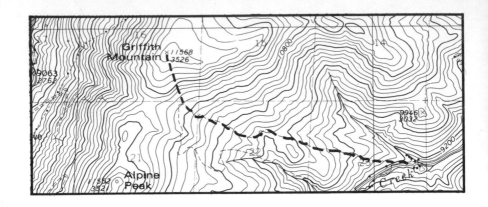

42. Horsetooth Peak 10,344 feet

Hike Distance: 2.2 miles each way
Hiking Time: Up in 110 minutes. Down in 68 minutes.
Starting Elevation: 8,740 feet
Elevation Gain: 1,604 feet
Difficulty: Moderate (requiring some moderate hand work over rock at the summit).
Trail: Total except for the last 124 feet (from the saddle).
Relevant Maps: Allens Park 7½ minute
Boulder County
Rocky Mountain National Park
Roosevelt National Forest
Views from the summit: S to Lookout Mountain
SSW to Meadow Mountain
W to Mount Orton
WNW to Mount Meeker.

Comment:

Horsetooth Peak is named for the configuration of its summit. No Rocky Mountain National Park fee is required for this route. The distinctive summit boulder may prove unnegotiable for the solo hiker. A second person can provide the necessary support.

Directions to the trailhead:

Drive on Colorado 7 either 12.0 miles south from U.S. 36 in Estes Park or 22.3 miles north on Colorado 7 from the junction with U.S. 36 in Lyons to Meeker Park. Opposite the Meeker Park Lodge is Colorado Road 113 going west past some cabins. This dirt road has a "Dead End" sign at its beginning. Follow this road west a total of 0.7 miles where it ends near a cabin. En route avoid side roads to cabins and stay on the well maintained main road. Park off the road.

The Hike:

Unmarked trails pass east and west from where you have parked at road end. Take the trail west and in a minute you enter Rocky Mountain National Park at a sign. Continue on the trail for about eight minutes with Horse Creek on your left until the trail clearly crosses the creek, rises and curves southwest and then south to reach a saddle between Horsetooth Peak on your left (northeast) and Lookout Mountain to your right, (southwest). Bushwhack up to the northeast from the saddle to a prominent unmarked rocky summit. To ascend the summit boulder is somewhat demanding and requires the use of hands. Descend by way of your ascent route.

Horsetooth Peak from the southwest

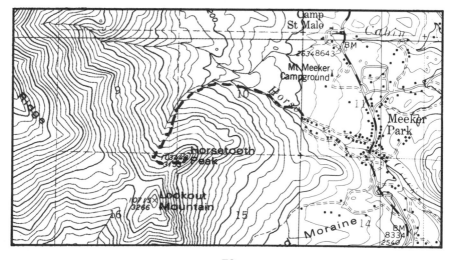

43. Red Mountain 12,315 feet (Clear Creek County)

Hike Distance: 1.2 miles each way (loop)
Hiking Time: Up in 90 minutes. Down in 75 minutes.
Starting Elevation: 10,115 feet
Elevation Gain: 2,200 feet
Difficulty: Moderate (steepness and some easy hand work may be needed on the rocky traverse just before the summit)
Trail: None
Relevant Maps: Berthoud Pass 7½ minute
Clear Creek County
Arapaho National Forest
Views from the summit: NNE to Stoney Mountain
NE to Colorado Mines Peak and Berthoud Pass
NW to Vasquez Peak
E to Engelmann Peak
ESE to Robeson Peak
S to Woods Mountain
SE to Bard Peak and Mount Parnassus
W to Jones Pass, Bobtail Mountain and the Henderson Mine

Comment:

Red Mountain, one of several in Colorado, is a prominent, pyramidal peak to the southwest on the south side of Berthoud Pass. This hike requires bushwhacking all the way to timberline but the summit ridge is visible for virtually the entire route. The Urad Mine at its southern base processed largely molybdenum and closed in 1974.

Directions to trailhead:

Drive west on U.S. 40 from Main Street in the town of Empire (toward Berthoud Pass) for 7.4 miles or drive 5.9 miles on U.S. 40 south from Berthoud Pass. Then turn west off the main road at the Big Bend Picnic Area sign and drive 0.4 miles west to a fork. Take the left fork toward the Urad Mine and drive southwest for 1.05 miles or so and park off the road in a large, open, flat area. Red Mountain is visible to the west.

The Hike:

Cross the flat area to the west and ascend quite steeply into the couloir. As you gain altitude, cross an old mining road and continue west and up until you reach the northeast ridge of Red Mountain. Continue up and to the southwest along the ridge and reach timberline. Continue past some old mine ruins and ascend a talus slope to a false summit. Continue over an easy rocky traverse, staying mostly to the west, to the summit cairn, a red and white metal pole and a register cylinder. Hands may occasionally be necessary as you negotiate the rocky traverse before the summit but there is no special risk or danger. The best descent is the way you came up. However, if you want variety, you may descend steeply from the saddle between the true and false summits east into the couloir to the southwest of the one in which you ascended. This connects eventually with an old mining road which brings you down southwest of the abandoned Urad Mine buildings and your car.

Red Mountain from U.S. 40 north of Empire

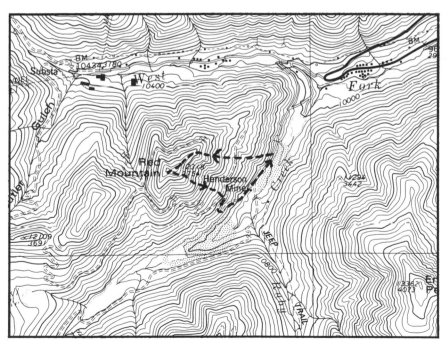

44. Estes Cone   11,006 feet

Hike Distance: 3.0 miles each way
Hiking Time: Up in 87 minutes. Down in 80 minutes.
Starting Elevation: 9,400 feet
Elevation Gain: 2,206 feet (includes 300 feet of extra elevation gain each
                     way)
Difficulty: Moderate
Trail: All the way until the rocky top.
Relevant Maps: Longs Peak 7½ minute
                     Larimer County Number Three
                     Rocky Mountain National Park
Views from the summit: N to Lake Estes
                     NNE to Lily Mountain
                     NW to Ypsilon Mountain and the Mummy Range
                     E to Twin Sisters Peaks
                     SSW to Mount Meeker
                     SW to Longs Peak and Battle Mountain

Comment:

This peak is prominent from Colorado 7 in the Longs Peak area. It is named
after Joel Estes, who is said to have been the first settler in what is now
called Estes Park. No Rocky Mountain National Park admission fee is required for this hike.

Directions to the trailhead:

Drive north from Lyons on Colorado 7 from its junction with U.S. 36 for 25.1
miles or south from Estes Park on Colorado 7 from its junction with U.S. 36
for 9.2 miles. Turn west at the sign to Longs Peak Campground and drive
for 1.1 miles to the parking area at road end at the Longs Peak Ranger
Station and the trailhead.

The Hike:

Begin south on the excellent trail from the Longs Peak Ranger Station. Pass
a trail register and turn northwest through the trees by trail to a fork which
is a half mile from the trailhead. Go to the right and past the ruins of the
Eugenia Mine in 0.9 more miles. Continue north on the trail and descend
into Moore Park. A corral and fork are reached 0.6 miles from the Eugenia
Mine. Ascend the left fork to the north northwest and after a steeper six
tenths of a mile reach a rock pile at a final fork. Take the right fork to the
north and follow a fainter trail and a series of cairns as the going becomes
steeper. At the rocky summit block follow the trail and cairns through a notch.
Then descend briefly before the final ascent to a large rock pile on top of
the Estes Cone. Some easy hand work may be needed. Enjoy the vistas;
especially over to Mount Meeker and Longs Peak. Be careful to retrace your
ascent route and follow the cairns down to the rock pile and take the left fork.

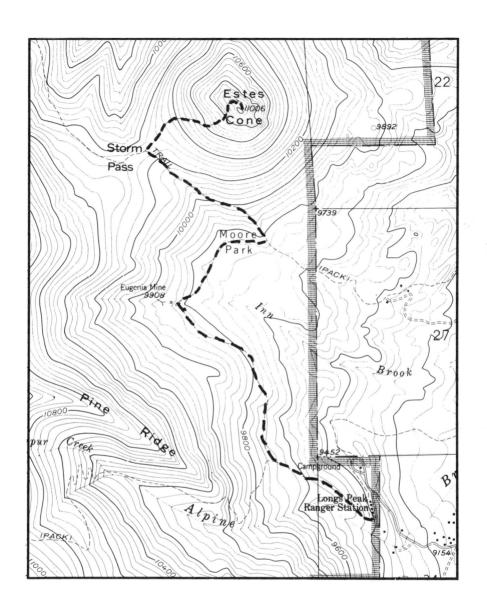

45. Vasquez Peak 12,947 feet

Hike Distance: 2.0 miles each way (loop)
Hiking Time: Up in 107 minutes. Down in 55 minutes.
Starting Elevation: 10,440 feet
Elevation Gain: 2,507 feet
Difficulty: Moderate
Trail: Only for initial 0.33 miles.
Relevant Maps: Berthoud Pass 7½ minute
                      Clear Creek County
                      Arapaho National Forest
Views from the summit: NNE to Longs Peak, Mount Meeker and North and
                      South Arapaho Peaks.
                      NE to James Peak
                      E to Stanley Mountain, Colorado Mines Peak and
                      Mount Flora
                      SSE to Grays Peak and Torreys Peak
                      SE to Engelmann Peak, Robeson Peak, Bard Peak
                      and Mount Parnassus.
                      SW to Jones Pass, Bobtail Mountain and
                      Pettingell Peak
                      W to Mount Nystrom
                      WNW to Bills Peak and Byers Peak

Comment:

This mountain is named after Louis Vasquez, one of the earliest settlefs of
Colorado. Vasquez was a hunter, explorer and fur trader. It is believed that
he built the first cabin in Clear Creek County. Vasquez Peak lies on the Continental Divide and forms part of the boundary between Clear Creek and
Grand Counties.

Directions to the trailhead:

Drive west on U.S. 40 from its junction with I-70 for 9.6 miles passing
through the town of Empire and turn left (west) at the bend in the road
before it rises to Berthoud Pass. This turn off lies 5.9 miles south of Berthoud Pass. Continue west on this paved road, bypassing a left fork at 0.4
miles, for a total of 1.75 miles to the Henderson Mine entrance where a dirt
road goes off to the right and ascends to Jones Pass. Drive northwest up
this road for 1.45 miles to some old ruins on the right just before the road
crosses the creek. Park off the road to the right. Many regular cars can drive
this far.

The Hike:

Follow the old mining road to the north northeast for one third of a mile until it ends. Then turn right (northeast) and ascend steeply through a bare
area with a few dead trees. About 33 minutes from the trailhead you will
reach timberline. Turn left (north) and cross boulders, scree and tundra
along the base of a false summit to your right (east). When you reach the
drainage, turn right (northeast) and ascend to the saddle. Turn left (northwest) at the saddle and ascend the ridge and gain the summit in eleven
minutes or so. A large cairn and a register jar mark the top. To descend,
return to the saddle and descend the drainage to the southwest until
around timberline. At timberline go directly south (left) angling through the

trees back to the trailhead and complete the loop. If you prefer less tree cover and a less gradual loss of elevation, follow your ascent route.

Vasquez Peak summit from the south

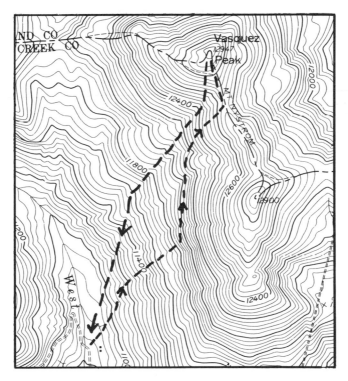

46. Caribou Peak 12,310 feet

Hike Distance: 3.7 miles each way
Hiking Time: Up in 115 minutes. Down in 85 minutes.
Starting Elevation: 9,960 feet
Elevation Gain: 2,400 feet (includes 25 feet of extra elevation gain each way)
Difficulty: Moderate
Trail: All the way to 100 feet from the top.
Relevant Maps: Ward 7½ minute
                     Boulder County
                     Roosevelt National Forest
Views from the summit: NNW to Kiowa Peak, Mount Albion and
                     Mount Audubon
                     NE to Niwot Mountain
                     ESE to Barker Reservoir
                     SSE to Lake Eldora Ski Area
                     SE to Nederland
                     WNW to North Arapaho Peak

Comment:

This mountain is named after the nearby, former Caribou Mine and the present ghost town of Caribou. Silver was mined in this area. The town of Caribou had as many as three thousand residents in the mid 1870s.

Directions to the trailhead:

From Nederland, drive west and then north on Colorado Road 72 for 7.25 miles and turn left (south) onto Colorado Road 116 which is also National Forest Road 505. Follow this rough road southwest for 5.2 miles through the Rainbow Lakes Campground to a parking area on your right just below and to the northeast of the parking area at the end of the road at the Rainbow Lakes Trailhead. Park here. Regular cars should be able to drive this far. En route to the trailhead on Colorado Road 116, keep left at 0.85 miles and right after 3.55 more miles.

The Hike:

The trail begins at the left side of the parking area at a sign stating, "Glacier Rim Trail, Arapaho Glacier Overlook, 6 (miles), Arapaho Pass Trail, 8 (miles)". Follow this clear trail generally north and then west as it rises above timberline along the boundary of the Boulder Watershed and then up the northern flank of Caribou Peak. About 100 feet below the top, leave the trail and ascend south to a huge cairn with an embedded metal pole. The only other marker on the summit is a small adjacent cairn. Descend by your ascent route unless you want the variety of a loop. (First descend southeast and then northeast to the Rainbow Lakes where a trail runs back to the trailhead and your vehicle.)

Caribou Peak from one of the Rainbow lakes

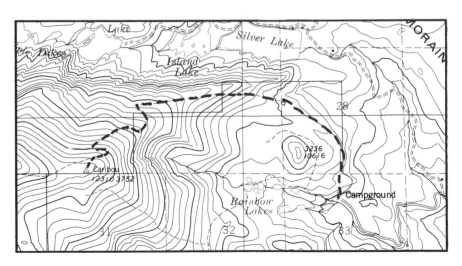

47. Mount Trelease 12,477 feet

Hike Distance: 2.65 miles each way
Hiking Time: Up in 125 minutes. Down in 95 minutes.
Starting Elevation: 10,720 feet
Elevation Gain: 1,757 feet
Difficulty: Moderate
Trail: First half
Relevant Maps: Loveland Pass 7½ minute
                   Clear Creek County
                   Arapaho National Forest
Views from the summit: N to Citadel Peak (the unofficially named 13,294
                   foot peak between Hagar Mountain and
                   Pettingell Peak).
                   NE to Mount Bethel
                   NW to Hagar Mountain
                   ESE to Grays Peak and Torreys Peak

Comment:

The Eisenhower-Johnson Tunnel was cut through the southwestern flank of Mount Trelease. Its summit overlooks the Loveland Basin Ski Area to the south and Loveland Valley Ski Area to the southeast.

Directions to the trailhead:

From I-70 between Bakerville and the Eisenhower-Johnson Tunnel, take Exit 216 and park on the north side of I-70 as the exit road begins to curve and pass south under I-70. A neglected access road which is blocked to vehicles begins where you have parked and passes to the northeast.

The Hike:

Proceed around the barrier and follow the access road northeast. You will pass two other barriers as the road rises, curves north and then northwest and enters Dry Gulch. Hike about 0.4 miles further northwest after the road ends, keeping to the right of the creek. There is no trail from here onward. At about 11,000 feet turn southwest, cross the creek and ascend Mount Trelease directly for about one mile during which you will gain about 1500 feet. The summit is visible to the right of a smaller subpeak. The top has no special marking. Take the same route back to the trailhead.

Mount Bethel from Mount Trelease

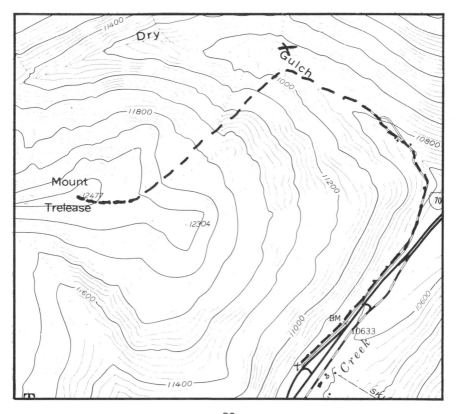

48. Grizzly Peak 13,427 feet

Hike Distance: 2.6 miles each way
Hiking Time: Up in 122 minutes. Down in 95 minutes.
Starting Elevation: 11,990 feet (Loveland Pass)
Elevation Gain: 2,387 feet (includes 475 feet of extra elevation gain each way)
Difficulty: Moderate
Trail: Virtually all the way with occasional gaps
Relevant Maps: Grays Peak 7½ minute
Clear Creek County
Arapaho National Forest
Views from the summit: N to Mount Parnassus
NNE to Bard Peak
NNW to Mount Sniktau and Woods Mountain
NE to Baker Mountain and Republican Mountain
NW to Coon Hill, Hagar Mountain and
Pettingell Peak
E to Torreys Peak
ENE to Ganley Mountain and Kelso Mountain
ESE to Grays Peak
S to Lenawee Mountain
SSE to Chihuahua Lake
SSW to Mount Guyot, Boreas Mountain and Bald
Mountain
SE to Square Top Mountain
SW to Quandary Peak, the Tenmile Range,
Keystone Ski Area, Lake Dillon and Mount of the
Holy Cross.

Comment:

This is a great hike for those who enjoy ridge walking above timberline. Grizzly Peak and much of this hike are on the Continental Divide and the boundary between Clear Creek County and Summit County.

Directions to the trailhead:

Drive to Loveland Pass on U.S. 6 either south from Interstate 70 via Exit 216 or west from Dillon and Keystone. Park at the pass off of the east side of the road.

The Hike:

Proceed up the ridge to the northeast on a clear trail. In about 25 minutes leave this trail and turn right (southeast) before you reach the ridge. A trail passes in this direction but is not essential to the hike. Eventually reach the ridge and continue southeast. You will lose elevation as you pass over or near several unnamed high points. The final saddle on the ridge lies 660 feet below the Grizzly Peak summit. A trail is present for most of the ridge and is very distinct over scree for the final ascent. At the top is a semi-open rock shelter. The summit ridge extends toward Torreys Peak to the east. The routes up Torreys from this point and from Chihuahua Gulch to the southeast appear relatively easy. Descend by your ascent route back to Loveland Pass which can be seen throughout most of the hike.

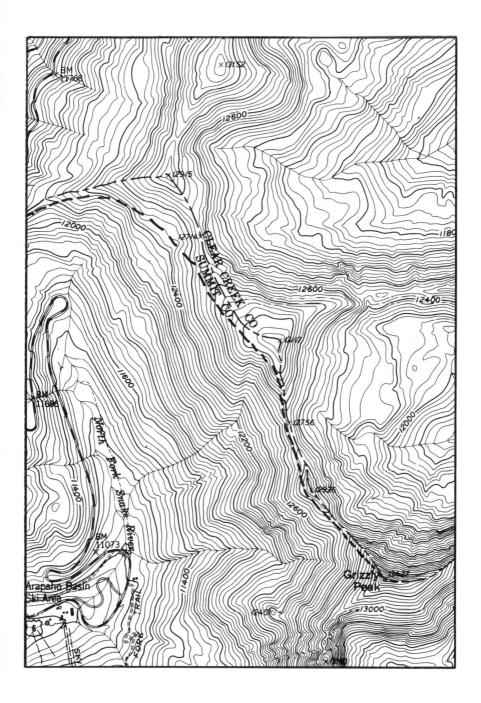

49. Mount Bethel 12,705 feet

Hike Distance: 2.8 miles on the ascent. 2.3 miles on the descent (loop)
Hiking Time: Up in 125 minutes. Down in 105 minutes.
Starting Elevation: 10,720 feet
Elevation Gain: 1,985 feet
Difficulty: Moderate (due to steepness)
Trail: For the initial half of the ascent and the latter half of the descent
Relevant Maps: Loveland Pass 7½ minute
                   Clear Creek County
                   Arapaho National Forest
Views from the summit: N to Vasquez Peak
                   NE to Mount Parnassus and Bard Peak
                   SE to Mount Sniktau
                   W to Citadel Peak (unofficial name), Hagar
                   Mountain and Pettingell Peak

Comment:

Formerly called Little Professor Peak, Mount Bethel was renamed after Ellsworth Bethel, a pathologist with the U.S. Department of Agriculture, who was very involved with the Rockies.

The triangular top of this mountain dominates the western horizon as one drives from Bakerville on I-70 toward Loveland Basin. Mount Bethel lies between Dry Gulch to the southeast and Herman Gulch to the northeast.

Directions to the trailhead:

Drive on I-70 between Bakerville and the Eisenhower-Johnson Tunnel. Take exit 216 and park on the north side of I-70 at a frontage road running to the northeast.

The Hike:

Walk northeast on the frontage road as it ascends and curves north and then northwest into Dry Gulch. The road is blocked to vehicles at three places but accessible on foot.

As you enter the basin, Mount Bethel will be visible on your right and is distinguishable by two rows of snow barricades on its southwest flank. At road end, keep a few hundred yards to the right of Dry Creek and soon begin to hike up and north toward the saddle to the west of Mount Bethel. Before you reach the saddle, angle steeply northeast, gain the ridge and proceed to the cairn at the summit. Some easy hand work may be necessary just before the ridge but there is no special risk. The descent can be made more directly due south to the place where the road ended on your ascent.

Mount Bethel from Interstate 70, east of the Eisenhower-Johnson Tunnel

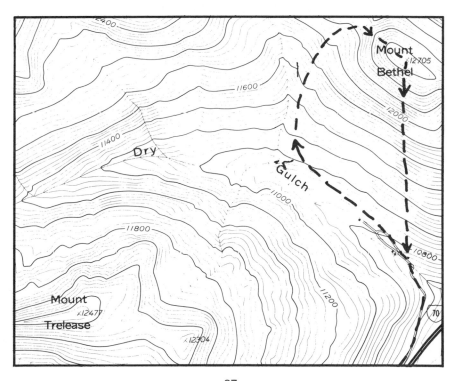

50. Bergen Peak 9,708 feet

Hike Distance:	4.6 miles each way
Hiking Time:	Up in 120 minutes. Down in 80 minutes.
Starting Elevation:	7,760 feet
Elevation Gain:	2,708 feet (includes an extra 380 feet each way)
Difficulty:	Moderate
Trail:	All the way
Relevant Maps:	Squaw Pass 7½ minute
	Evergreen 7½ minute
	Jefferson County Number One
	Elk Meadow Park Map (Jefferson County Open Space).

Views from the summit: NW to Saddleback Mountain
S to Krinder Peak
SSE to Pikes Peak
E to Mount Morrison and Mount Falcon
SW to Mount Evans
W to Mount Pence, Snyder Mountain, Chief
Mountain & Squaw Mountain

Comment:

Bergen Peak is named after Thomas C. Bergen who came from Illinois seeking gold and settled west of Denver in 1859. His combined hotel and post office was a busy spot along the toll road west from Mount Vernon. He was one of the first three Jefferson County Commissioners.

This makes a good early (April) or late (November) season hike and is well marked with signs. There are several other trails in this Jefferson County Park, which is free and open to the public.

Directions to the trailhead:

Either drive south from Bergen Park on Colorado 74 from its junction with Colorado 103 for 2.5 miles or drive north from Evergreen on Colorado 74 from its junction with Jefferson County 73 for 2.1 miles. Then turn west onto Stage Coach Boulevard and in 1.1 miles park on the right (north) in the trailhead parking area.

The Hike:

Proceed to the northeast on a trail past picnic tables and toilets to a junction in 0.3 miles. Take the left fork and continue along the Meadow View Trail for 0.6 miles. Then at another fork go left again and head west and then northwest on the Bergen Peak Trail for 2.7 miles where yet another left fork leads you in a counterclockwise route of one more mile to the Bergen Peak summit. The trail passes a scenic overlook and gets a bit faint later near the summit. You pass a wooden shack and a radio tower just before reaching the top which is marked by a wooden elevation sign. Take the same route back or if you want more exercise or variety, at the first trail intersection one mile down from the summit, take the left fork onto the Too Long Trail which eventually curves around to connect with the beginning segments of your ascent route.

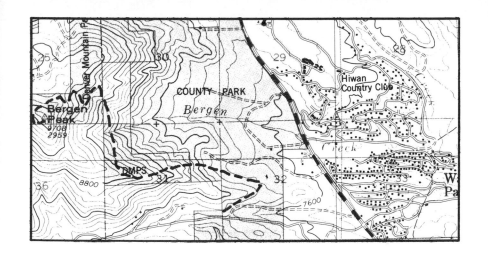

51. Raleigh Peak 8,183 feet

Hike Distance: 3.4 miles each way
Hiking Time: Up in 113 minutes. Down in 85 minutes.
Starting Elevation: 7,760 feet
Elevation Gain: 2,243 feet (includes 70 extra feet each way)
Difficulty: Moderate (some easy rock scrambling near the top)
Trail: Initial 2.8 miles and faint intermittent trail thereafter.
Relevant Maps: Platte Canyon 7½ minute
                  Jefferson County Number Two
                  Pike National Forest
Views from the summit: SSE to Long Scraggy Peak and Cheesman Mountain
                  SSW to Little Scraggy Peak and Green Mountain
                  SE to Devils Head
                  SW to Windy Peak
                  WNW to Chair Rocks, Mount Evans and Cathedral
                  Spires

Comment:

This is a good early or late season hike with an impressive, rocky summit. The route, after leaving the road, requires some bushwhacking and compass work. The proposed Two Forks Reservoir would submerge the initial part of this hike. (This peak may also be reached from the southwest via Jefferson County Road 126.) Parts of this route are used heavily by motorbikers.

Directions to the trailhead:

Drive southwest on U.S. 285 through Aspen Park and Conifer and turn south onto Jefferson County Road 97 which passes through Reynolds Park. After 8.3 miles from U.S. 285, turn left at a fork at the South Platte River. Then drive 5.7 miles along the left side of the river and turn right just before you reach the abandoned South Platte Hotel. Cross the metal bridge and park off the road. (Four wheel drive is needed beyond.)

The Hike:

Ascend the road to the southwest and pass a Colorado trail sign on your right. Follow the main road as it rises to the southwest and west. After about 1.5 miles Raleigh Peak will come into view. After another 1.3 miles keep right at two successive forks and reach a semi-open area with trails to the left and right and the main road continuing ahead around a solitary tree. Leave the road here and bushwhack 150 degrees southeast directly toward Raleigh Peak. As you ascend you may find a faint trail. Proceed toward the right side of the rocky summit and pick your way to the top. Some easy hand work will be needed. The summit contains some old wood and wire with a U.S.G.S. marker nearby. Use your compass to retrace your route back to the trailhead.

Raleigh Peak from the northeast

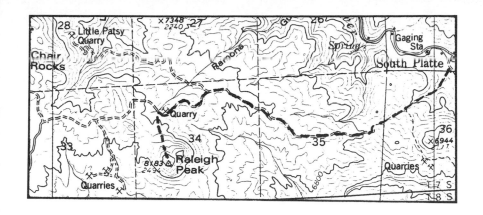

52. Resolution Mountain 11,905 feet

Hike Distance: 3.0 miles each way
Hiking Time: Up in 120 minutes. Down in 70 minutes via the ascent
                     route or down in 60 minutes by the loop route south
                     from the summit to the Resolution Road.
Starting Elevation: 9,678 feet
Elevation Gain: 2,227 feet
Difficulty: Moderate
Trail: First two miles
Relevant Maps: Pando 7½ minute
                     Eagle County Number Four
                     White River National Forest
Views from the summit: NE to Shrine Mountain
                     ENE to Ptarmigan Hill
                     SW to Mount of the Holy Cross
                     WNW to Hornsilver Mountain

Comment:

To reach the trailhead one must pass through the ruins of Camp Hale which
was established to train ski troops of the U.S. Army 10th Mountain Division
for World War II and also as a camp for German prisoners of war.

When the Resolution Road Number 702 is open to motor vehicles, this hike
can be two miles shorter each way since regular cars can then drive to the
point at 10,382 feet where the route leaves the road and goes northwest.
These directions are from the place where the road is often blocked.

Directions to the trailhead:

Drive south of Leadville on U.S. 24 from its intersection with Colorado 91 for
14.8 miles. Or if you come from the north, drive 15.2 miles south on U.S. 24
from Minturn. Either of these routes brings you to a turnoff to the east
through two stone pillars into the former site of Camp Hale. After pro-

ceeding off U.S. 24 through these pillars 0.2 miles, turn left at a T and drive for 0.9 miles to a turnoff to the right and a creek crossing. You are now on Resolution Road Number 702. Keep on this road as it ascends northeast alongside Resolution Creek for 1.9 miles to a fork. The left fork is what you want and is often blocked to vehicles at this point. Park here.

The Hike:

Continue northeast on foot up the road to the left along Resolution Creek for about two miles where the road turns sharply to the right (east). Leave the road at this sharp bend and ascend up the gulch going northwest and keeping to the left of the creek. Stay left at the confluence of two creeks, continue northwest and gain the ridge at a low point and then turn left (south) to the summit which lies a total of one mile from where you left the Resolution Road. At the top there is a metal pole marker and a nearby cement slab with two embedded metal rods. To descend you may retrace your route or make a loop by descending south to the unnamed creek which passes east through the aspens by way of an abandoned mine to the Resolution Road. (N.B. If the Resolution Road is open to vehicles, a regular car can ascend to the sharp bend in the road at 10,382 feet and the hike can begin there and continue northwest up the gulch away from the road. This would save 2 miles and 704 feet of elevation on the ascent.)

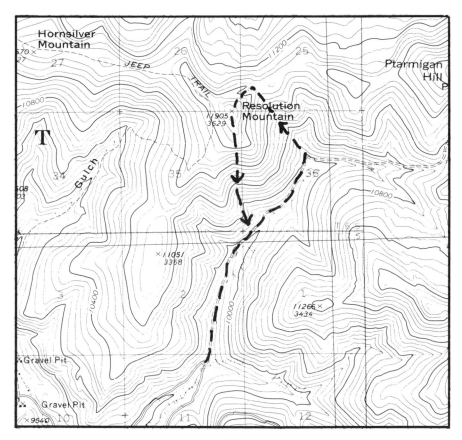

53. Bald Mountain 13,684 feet

Hike Distance:	2.0 miles each way
Hiking Time:	Up in 130 minutes. Down in 90 minutes.
Starting Elevation:	11,390 feet
Elevation Gain:	2,602 feet (includes 154 feet lost between false summits).
Difficulty:	Moderate
Trail:	None
Relevant Maps:	Boreas Pass 7½ minute
	Summit County Number Two
	Arapaho National Forest
Views from the summit:	E to South Park
	ENE to Mount Guyot
	SSE to Boreas Mountain
	SSW to Mount Silverheels
	W to the Tenmile Range

Comment:

This is a good hike for those who enjoy ridge walking and being above timberline.

Before its final name after the God of the North Wind, Boreas Pass had been called Hamilton, Tarryall and then Breckenridge Pass. In 1882, track was laid over the pass and it was a Denver, South Park and Pacific Railroad Company route until 1937. A town called Boreas was located at the pass for the railroad workers and travelers.

Directions to the trailhead:

Drive to the south end of the town of Breckenridge on U.S. 9 and turn east onto the Boreas Pass Road. Drive on the road 9.65 miles toward the pass. Park at the bend in the road 0.6 miles short of the pass. From the southeast Boreas Pass can be reached by turning west off U.S. 285 at Como and driving through Como for a total of 11.3 miles to the pass. The trailhead is 0.6 miles further north beyond the pass. Regular cars can traverse Boreas Pass when there is no blockage by snow. Park off the road.

The Hike:

Head northeast and up staying to the left of the creek and quickly pass timberline. Proceed to the ridge at the left of the saddle between Bald Mountain on your left and Boreas Mountain on your right. Ascend this ridge and traverse several false summits as you head north. The true summit is marked by a large cairn and a circular rock shelter. Two other large cairns lie further to the northwest down from the summit. To descend, stay on the summit ridge and keep to the west (right) of the last two false summits and return as you came up.

Bald Mountain from Boreas Mountain

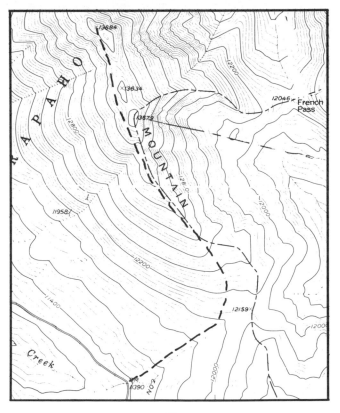

54. Hornsilver Mountain 11,572 feet

Hike Distance: 4.0 miles each way
Hiking Time: Up in 120 minutes. Down in 100 minutes.
Starting Elevation: 9,020 feet
Elevation Gain: 2,552 feet
Difficulty: Moderate
Trail: All the way
Relevant Maps: Red Cliff 7½ minute
                     Pando 7½ minute
                     Eagle County Number Four
                     White River National Forest
Views from the summit: N to the Gore Range
                     NE to Uneva Peak
                     E to Pacific Peak, Ptarmigan Hill and Resolution
                     Mountain
                     ENE to Shrine Pass and Shrine Mountain
                     S to Camp Hale and Mount Massive
                     SSE to Buckeye Peak
                     SSW to Homestake Peak
                     SE to Mount Sherman
                     SW to the Homestake Reservoir, Whitney Peak,
                     Mount of the Holy Cross and Notch Mountain

Comment:

Hornsilver's flat, grassy summit affords excellent views of the Mount of the Holy Cross. Four wheel drive can take you to the top of Hornsilver Mountain and also to near the top of adjacent Resolution Mountain to the south by way of the same road. For easier crossings of Wearyman Creek this hike is best done in late August or September.

Directions to the trailhead:

From Redcliff drive east on the Shrine Pass Road for 2.45 miles or from the Shrine Pass cutoff of Interstate 70 drive west over Shrine Pass toward Redcliff for a total of 8.5 miles from I-70. Park here off the road as four wheel drive is needed beyond this point for the side road to Hornsilver Mountain.

The Hike:

Leave the Shrine Pass Road and go south on Road 747. Follow this rough road for 0.65 miles crossing Wearyman Creek at several points and take the right fork onto Road 708. Follow this road up and generally south in a counterclockwise direction to the flat grassy summit at timberline. A few rocks, old boards and wire mark the high point just west of the road. Return by the same route.

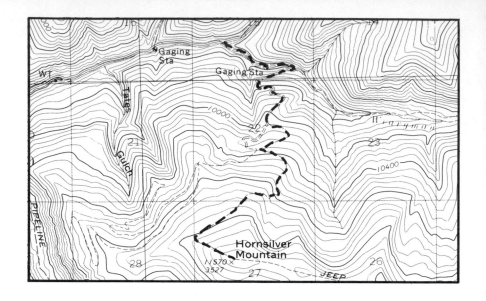

55. Twin Cones 12,060 and 12,058 feet

Hike Distance: 4.0 miles each way
Hiking Time: Up in 120 minutes to the southern Cone. Over to the nor-
                    thern Cone in 20 minutes and back in 115 minutes.
Starting Elevation: 11,315 feet
Elevation Gain: 1,645 feet (includes 340 feet of extra elevation gain on
                    the ascent and 560 feet on the return).
Difficulty: Moderate
Trail: Initial 1.5 miles
Relevant Maps: Berthoud Pass 7½ minute
                    Grand County Number Four
                    Arapaho National Forest
Views from the summits: NNE to Mount Epworth
                    NNW to Winter Park (from northern Cone)
                    NE to James Peak
                    NW to Fraser (from northern Cone)
                    E to Mount Flora
                    S to Engelmann Peak and Mount Parnassus
                    SE to Colorado Mines Peak
                    SW to Stanley Mountain, Vasquez Peak,
                    Mount Nystrom
                    W to Byers Peak and Bottle Peak

Comment:

This is a leisurely ridge walk partly along the Continental Divide. The west
side of Berthoud Pass has less named and less impressive peaks then the
eastern ridge.

Directions to the trailhead:

Drive to Berthoud Pass on U.S. 40 between Empire to the south and Winter Park to the north. Park off the road. There is abundant parking area.

The Hike:

Ascend the rough road to the west southwest from 100 yards south of Berthoud Pass. A barrier may prevent vehicular access to this road. After 0.7 miles on this road you will reach a ridge at the end of the ski lift at timberline. Follow the faint trail up to the west and a mesa. Numerous large cairns mark the trail which is part of the Continental Divide Trail. Turn right (north) at the mesa and follow a faint trail north to two conical projections. These cones are 0.5 miles apart. Each high point is marked only by a few loose rocks. The return is a little more demanding due to elevation gain and does not offer as clearly visible a destination. Keep south southwest until you reach the ridge going east back to the trailhead.

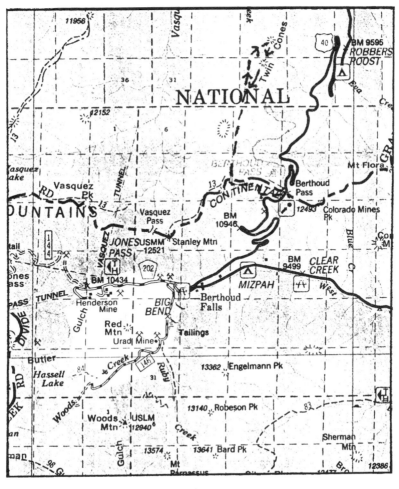

56. Jaque Peak 13,205 feet

Hike Distance: 4.1 miles to summit. 1.4 miles back to trailhead (loop)
Hiking Time: Up in 145 minutes. Down in 55 minutes.
Starting Elevation: 10,980 feet
Elevation Gain: 2,225 feet
Difficulty: Moderate
Trail: From trailhead to Searle Pass and east to around the
                   subpeak.
Relevant Maps: Copper Mountain 7½ minute
                   Summit County Number Two
                   Arapaho National Forest
Views from the summit: NE to Union Mountain and Copper Mountain
                   E to Tucker Mountain and the Tenmile Range
                   SW to Corbett Peak
                   W to Elk Mountain

Comment:

This peak is named after Captian J.C. Jaque, a well-known character who lived in Leadville and died there in 1890.

Directions to the trailhead:

Drive south from I-70 at Copper Mountain toward Leadville on Colorado 91 for 4.0 miles. Or drive north from Fremont Pass on Colorado 91 for 7.45 miles. Turn off Colorado 91 onto a paved road going northwest for 0.9 miles. Then take the dirt road going to your right and ascend northwest for 3.4 miles. Park at an open area on your left at a sign saying, "Searle Pass Parking Area." The road is passible for regular cars.

The Hike:

Cross the road and head northwest up an old mining road into Searle Gulch. Continue on this road until it disappears in scrub oak. Then follow the pink ribbons on the trees directing you toward Searle Pass which is the lowest point on your right to the northwest. From the pass follow a trail going east up over grassy slopes to the right of a subpeak to the impressive true high point which is marked by a cairn and a simple jar register. It will take about 90 minutes from Searle Pass to the Jaque Peak summit. Descend directly downward steeply southwest over tundra and then through the trees to your vehicle which will be visible from the top of the peak.

Jaque Peak from the south

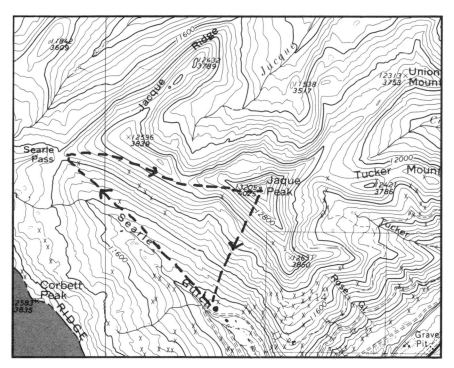

57. Quail Mountain 13,461 feet

Hike Distance: 3.1 miles each way
Hiking Time: Up in 140 minutes. Down in 90 minutes.
Starting Elevation: 9,870 feet
Elevation Gain: 2,720 feet (includes 30 extra feet each way)
Difficulty: Moderate
Trail: All the way to the saddle at 12,530 feet
Relevant Maps: Mount Elbert 7½ minute
                    Winfield 7½ minute
                    Chaffee County Number One
                    San Isabel National Forest
                    Colorado Trail Map Number 11
Views from the summit: N to Twin Lakes
                    NW to Twin Peaks and Mount Elbert
                    E to Pikes Peak and the Buffalo Peaks
                    S to Huron Peak
                    SE to Waverly Mountain, Mount Oxford,
                    Mount Belford and Missouri Mountain
                    W to Mount Hope

Comment:

Quail Mountain is the location of a proposed ski area in the Twin Lakes area. This peak has a gentle rounded summit which provides extensive views of many high mountains. From the saddle to the west, Mount Hope is a 65 minute ridge hike.

Directions to the trailhead:

Drive west on Chaffee County Road 390 from US 24 between Leadville and Buena Vista. This road is 4.3 miles south of Colorado 82 and 15.3 miles north of the stop light in Buena Vista (at Colorado 306). On this good dirt road keep left at mile 3.5 and at mile 6.0. Pass the ghost town of Vicksburg at mile 8.0. Just past a pond and a camp site on the left at mile 9.4 the trailhead sign stating "Colorado Trail" will lie off the right side of the road. Park around here.

The Hike:

Begin north on the trail which leads steeply up into Sheep Gulch. On the way you will soon pass an abandoned mine shaft on the left and higher in the gulch an old cabin lies off the trail on your right. Around timberline the trail is marked by a series of cairns as it rises with switchbacks to the saddle between Mount Hope on your left (west) and Quail Mountain on your right (east). From this saddle at 12,530 feet leave the trail and ascend 0.7 miles east over tundra to the top of Quail Mountain. Descend as you ascended on the Colorado Trail.

Quail Mountain from the saddle

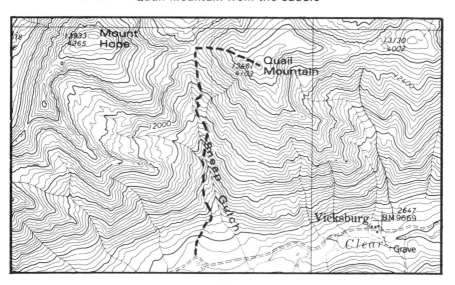

58. Mount Wilcox 13,408 feet and Otter Mountain 12,766 feet

Hike Distance: Trailhead to Mount Wilcox summit—1.95 miles. Mt. Wilcox summit to Otter Mountain summit—1.85 miles. Otter Mountain summit to trailhead—2.0 miles (loop).

Hiking Time: Up to Mount Wilcox in 116 minutes. Over to Otter Mountain in 46 minutes. Down in 68 minutes.

Elevation Gain: 2,394 feet

Difficulty: Moderate

Trail: Only the initial part across the valley.

Relevant Maps: Montezuma 7½ minute
Grays Peak 7½ minute
Georgetown 7½ minute
Clear Creek County
Arapaho National Forest

Views from the summit: **From Mount Wilcox**
NE to Otter Mountain and Sugarloaf Peak
E to Mount Evans, The Sawtooth and Mount Bierstadt
ESE to Naylor Lake
S to Square Top Mountain
SW to Argentine Peak
W to Torreys Peak, Grays Peak and Mount Edwards

From Otter Mountain
NE to Sugarloaf Peak
NW to Mount Parnassus and Bard Peak
ESE to Gray Wolf Mountain and Mount Spalding
SE to Mount Evans, The Sawtooth, Mount Bierstadt and Guanella Pass
SSW to Square Top Mountain
SW to Mount Wilcox and Argentine Peak
W to Torreys Peak, Mount Edwards and Grays Peak

Comment:

Mount Wilcox was named on August 1, 1948 after Edward John Wilcox who owned the nearby Waldorf Mines. In fact the ghost town of Waldorf was once called Wilcox. A railroad which ran up Mount McClellan opened on August 12, 1906 and passed through Waldorf which then was called the site of the highest post office in the United States. The train line could only operate three months out of each year and was eventually torn up in 1919.

Directions to the trailhead:

From the intersection of Sixth and Rose Streets in Georgetown, drive south and up toward Guanella Pass for 2.8 miles to a dirt road on your right. Turn off onto this road, take the right fork at 0.25 miles, another right fork at 0.5 miles and also at 1.0 miles from the paved road. In 0.2 miles further, take the sharp left fork and continue up the basin for a total of 6.25 miles from the Guanella Pass Road to the substantial ruins of the Waldorf Mine just above timberline and park. Most regular passenger cars can negotiate the road to this point. Mount Wilcox is the prominent peak to the southwest.

The Hike:

Go east over Leavenworth Creek to two abandoned cabins on the east side of the creek near some power lines. Follow an old mining road across the creek and through the marshes toward these cabins and thereby avoid most of the scrub oak on the basin floor. At the cabins the trail ends. Continue steeply up to the east and gain the ridge. This part will require about 84 minutes. Turn south on the ridge and soon the Mount Wilcox summit will come into view. Cross the tundra and ascend easily to a large cairn at the top. This will require about 32 minutes from the ridge.

Continue this loop hike down from Mount Wilcox and head northeast to Otter Mountain. Keep to the south of an unnamed peak with a rocky wind shelter on top. This peak lies about halfway between Mount Wilcox and Otter Mountain. Continue northeast over the gently rising tundra to another large cairn at the Otter Mountain summit. This will require about 46 minutes from the top of Mount Wilcox. Descend directly west to the ridge, then to the two cabins and across Leavenworth Creek to your car in about 68 minutes.

Mount Wilcox from Silver Dollar Lake

Argentine Peak from Mount Wilcox summit

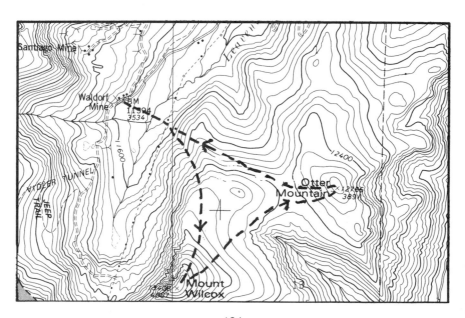

Mount Wilcox from Naylor Lake

59. Horseshoe Mountain 13,898 feet

Hike Distance: 3.1 miles each way
Hiking Time: Up in 145 minutes. Down in 95 minutes.
Starting Elevation: 11,480 feet
Elevation Gain: 2,418 feet
Difficulty: Moderate
Trail: All the way
Relevant Maps: Mount Sherman 7½ minute
                   Fairplay West 7½ minute
                   Park County Number One
                   Lake County
                   Pike National Forest
Views from the summit: N to Mount Sheridan, Peerless Mountain and
                   Mount Sherman

NE to the White Ridge (of Mount Sherman)
NW to Finnback Knob, Leadville and Turquoise Lake
E to Sheep Mountain and Lamb Mountain
S to Ptarmigan Peak
W to Mount Elbert and Mount Massive
WSW to Twin Lakes and the Collegiate Peaks

Comments:

As you drive west on the Fourmile Creek Road, you pass the site of the former town of Horseshoe which once had a population as much as 800 and was called East Leadville.

This hike lies totally above timberline and takes you through many abandoned mines to an extensive view from the summit which divides Park from Lake County. Horseshoe Mountain is named after its configuration.

Directions to the trailhead:

Drive south on U.S. 285 from Fairplay at the junction with Colorado 9 West for 1.25 miles. Then turn right (west) on Park County Road 18 (also called the Fourmile Creek Road) and continue up the valley on the main road for 11.3 miles to a 4-way intersection. Take the left (west) turn and stay to the left at the first fork and drive about 0.6 miles to around timberline and park off the road. Regular cars should be able to make it this far.

The Hike:

Continue on the road as it curls up west into Horseshoe Gulch. Horseshoe Mountain with its impressive cirque lies before you. Follow the road as it eventually angles northwest up to a ridge just south of Peerless Mountain. Evidence of abandoned mining efforts can be seen below and on this ridge. Then continue south on a gently ascending faint trail to a summit cairn and register cylinder. Return by the same route. (If you wish to hike up Peerless Mountain on your descent, it will add about 14 minutes and 168 feet of elevation gain to your outing.)

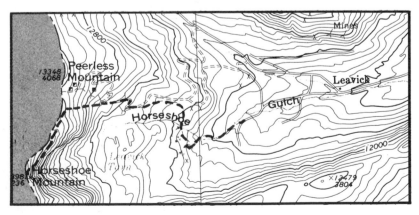

60. Sugarloaf Peak 12,513 feet

Hike Distance: 4.4 miles each way
Hiking Time: Up in 142 minutes. Down in 96 minutes.
Starting Elevation: 9,640 feet
Elevation Gain: 3,073 feet (includes 100 feet of extra elevation gain each way).
Difficulty: Moderate
Trail: Initial 2.8 miles
Relevant Maps: Georgetown 7½ minute
                     Clear Creek County
                     Arapaho National Forest
Views from the summit: NNE to Alpine Peak and to Griffith Mountain
                     NE to Lake Edith
                     NW to Mount Parnassus, Bard Peak, Silver Plume Mountain and Republican Mountain
                     SE to Hells Hole and Gray Wolf Mountain
                     SW to Square Top Mountain, Otter Mountain, Mount Wilcox and Argentine Peak
                     W to Upper Cabin Creek Reservoir
                     WNW to Ganley Mountain and Pendleton Mountain
                     WSW to Mount Edwards, Waldorf, McClellan Mountain and Torreys Peak

Comment:

Several Colorado Mountains are named Sugarloaf Peak due to its conical configuration. This peak can be seen from the northern segments of the Guanella Pass Road and from numerous Clear Creek County high points. Lake Edith to the northeast lies within private property. A loop return from the summit to the northeast via an old mining road and Lake Edith is therefore not recommended.

Directions to the trailhead:

From exit 240 off Interstate 70 at Idaho Springs, drive southwest on Colorado 103 for 6.7 miles. At a sharp bend in the road Road 114, also called the West Chicago Creek Road, leads southwest. Follow this excellent dirt road until it ends after 3.0 miles in a parking area just past the West Chicago Creek Campground. Park here.

The Hike:

The trail begins at a sign at the south end of the parking area. Follow this clear trail as it ascends to the south. After about 75 minutes, leave the trail and bushwhack west northwest to the saddle to the left (south) of Sugarloaf Peak. Ascend through sparse forest and eventually scrub oak to the ridge and then north northwest over tundra to the summit which is marked by a red and white pole embedded in a rockpile and a nearby U.S.G.S. marker in the midst of a smaller pile of rocks. Descend by your ascent route.

Sugarloaf Peak from the south

Sugarloaf Peak from West Chicago Creek Campground

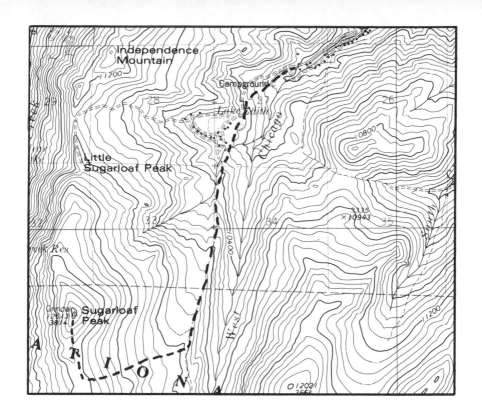

61. Whale Peak 13,078 feet

Hike Distance: 4.0 miles each way
Hiking Time: Up in 148 minutes. Down in 95 minutes.
Starting Elevation: 10,316 feet
Elevation Gain: 2,832 feet (includes 35 feet of extra elevation gain each way).
Difficulty: Moderate
Trail: All the way to Gibson Lake. Spotty above the lake until it resumes for the final half mile to the top.
Relevant Maps: Jefferson 7½ minute
Park County Number One
Pike National Forest
Views from the summit: NE to Handcart Peak, Red Cone and Mount Evans
SW to Boreas Mountain, Mount Guyot and
Glacier Peak
WNW to Sheep Mountain

Comment:

Whale Peak lies on the Continental Divide and the boundary between Park and Summit Counties and also between the Pike and Arapaho National

Forests. The Hall Valley is named after Colonel William Jairus Hall, a local mine owner.

Directions to the trailhead:

From U.S. 285 at the ghost town of Webster, (4.4 miles east of Kenosha Pass or 3.25 miles west of Grant), turn west on road 120 and drive up Hall Valley for 5.3 miles past the Handcart Campground to the Hall Valley Campground. En route take the right fork at 3.3. miles and the left fork at 5.2 miles from U.S. 285. Continue on the rough road up the valley for 1.25 miles past the Hall Valley Campground to a parking area on the left. Park here. Regular cars can make it this far.

The Hike:

Follow the trail which begins west of the parking area at a sign. Descend slightly to the south, cross the creek on a small wooden bridge and proceed southwest and then west up the valley on the clear trail which keeps to the right of the Lake Fork of the South Platte River until you cross it near timberline. In about 40 minutes from the trailhead, take the left fork and stay lower in the valley and closer to the creek. Avoid the right fork which ascends steeply into the northern edge of the basin. In about forty more minutes past the fork, you will arrive at Gibson Lake. If you lose the trail, just continue close to the creek and toward the southwest corner of the basin and Gibson Lake. Pass to the left of the lake and ascend talus and tundra to the south to gain a trail leading southwest past a false summit on your right and then north over tundra to a summit cairn. Descend as you came up.

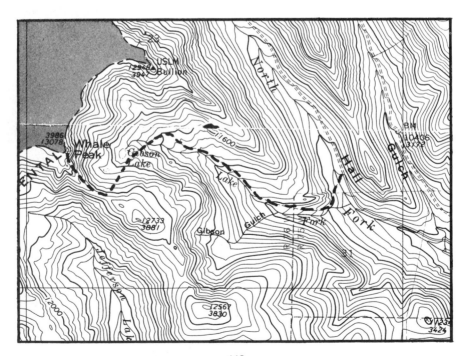

62. Mount Manitou 9,460 feet and Rocky Mountain 9,250 feet

Hike Distance: Trailhead to Mount Manitou summit 3.4 miles. Mount Manitou summit to Rocky Mountain summit 0.5 miles. Rocky Mountain summit to trailhead 3.3 miles (loop).

Hiking Time: Up to Mount Manitou in 120 minutes. Mount Manitou to Rocky Mountain in 33 minutes. Down from Rocky Mountain in 83 minutes (loop).

Starting Elevation: 6,680 feet

Elevation Gain: 2,820 feet to Mount Manitou (includes 40 extra feet of elevation gain). 90 feet more to Rocky Mountain. (Extra 150 feet on return.) Total 3,060 feet.

Difficulty: Moderate (some easy hand work needed at each summit)

Trail: All the way until the last 330 feet to Mount Manitou and the ridge between Mount Manitou and Rocky Mountain.

Relevant Maps: Manitou Springs 7½ minute
El Paso County Number One
Pike National Forest

Views from the summit: **From Mount Manitou**
E to Colorado Springs
SE to Cameron Cone
S to Sheep Mountain
SW to Pikes Peak

From Rocky Mountain
NW to Mount Manitou
E to Manitou Springs and Colorado Springs
SSE to Cameron Cone
SE to Cheyenne Mountain and Mount Arthur
SSW to Sheep Mountain
SW to Pikes Peak

Comment:

The first part of this loop hike involves the Barr Trail which is the major hiking route to Pikes Peak. This trail was completed by Fred Barr in 1921 and is extensively maintained. Manitou is an Algonquin Indian word meaning "great spirit."

Directions to the trailhead:

From Manitou Avenue in the town of Manitou Springs (west of Colorado Springs) drive southwest up Ruxton Avenue for 0.8 miles to the end of the public road. Turn right (northwest) and ascend 0.1 miles to a parking area, rest rooms and a bulletin board adjacent to the trail head. Park here.

The Hike:

Follow the Barr Trail steeply up and to the west in a series of switchbacks. The trail is very well maintained and has wooden fencing along it for most of the first two miles. After about 80 minutes, you will reach a fork. Continue to the left (west) on the Barr Trail. In about five more minutes, another fork at a metal sign is reached. Take the right fork toward the former Fremont Experimental Forest and leave the Barr Trail. After passing some old cement foundations on your right, in 17 minutes from the Barr Trail, you arrive at a saddle and a T. Take the right fork going northeast and ascend another 7 minutes before leaving the old road and proceeding due north to Mount Manitou.

Toward the top some easy scrambling is necessary. At the tree covered summit there is a large rock with a register jar on its top. To reach Rocky Mountain, descend toward the southeast and stay close to the ill-defined ridge. Cross the old road you had left earlier and continue generally east and upward past a false summit and reach the treeless, rocky top of Rocky Mountain with four embedded metal poles and a fixed wooden plank to assist you to ascend the summit boulder. Descend Rocky Mountain to the east and pick up a faint trail that winds past some rocky projections to reach the upper terminus of the Mount Manitou Incline Railway in about 15 minutes. (If you find no trail, just continue east.) From there take the trail west and upward 150 feet leading to the Barr Trail. After nine minutes, take the left fork, descend and reach the fork meeting the Barr Trail in 4 more minutes. Turn left (east) and descend on the trail on which you ascended and reach the trailhead in 55 minutes.

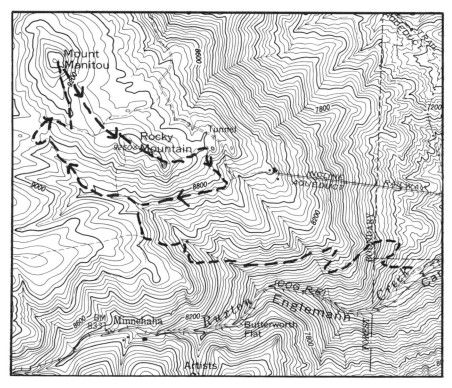

63. Buffalo Mountain 12,777 feet

Hike Distance: 1.8 miles each way
Hiking Time: Up in 150 minutes. Down in 90 minutes.
Starting Elevation: 9,560 feet
Elevation Gain: 3,217 feet
Difficulty: Moderate (steepness)
Trail: All the way to the talus slopes near the summit.
Relevant Maps: Frisco 7½ minute
                    Vail Pass 7½ minute
                    Summit County Number Two
                    Arapaho National Forest
Views from the summit: NE to Ptarmigan Peak
                    NW to Red Peak
                    E to Lake Dillon, Grays Peak and Torreys Peak
                    S to Peak 1
                    SE to Bald Mountain and Mount Guyot
                    SW to Uneva Peak

Comment:

There are a number of Buffalo Mountains in Colorado. This one is the dome which dominates the western view from the Eisenhower-Johnson Tunnel. The view of Lake Dillon and environs from the top is truly exceptional.

Directions to the trailhead:

From Interstate 70 take the Dillon-Silverthorne exit and drive northwest about one block and turn left (south) onto the Wildernest Road. Follow this road which becomes Ryan Gulch Road as it passes through an area of condominiums for 3.5 miles to the trailhead on the right (north) side of the road at a sign stating "Buffalo Cabin Trail." Park off the left (south) side of the road at a National Forest bulletin board.

The Hike:

Cross Ryan Gulch Road and proceed northwest on the Buffalo Cabin Trail. In 15 minutes take a left fork and a minute later you arrive at a 4-way intersection. A severe right turn takes you to Mesa Cortina. A milder right turn leads to Willow Creek. You will take the left turn which takes you past a ruined cabin on the right in twelve minutes and five minutes more to the ruined, so called, Buffalo Cabin. You now have a choice of two routes to the top of Buffalo Mountain. A trail to the left of Buffalo Cabin passes steeply up through the trees to the west over considerable scree and loose rocks. This trail ends above timberline as the summit comes into view on your left (south). Your other choice is a trail which begins at the right of Buffalo Cabin and continues northwest behind the cabin, is faint at times, passes under two large logs and eventually arrives at a lengthy, steep slope of talus and boulders on your left (west). Some easy hand work is needed as you ascend this slope. After the rocks you proceed up and southwest through more trees and then over a talus slope to reach the same point where the other trail leads above timberline. Be sure to keep left of the rocky crag. By either route it is about an hour hike from the Buffalo Cabin to the point above timberline where you can see the summit to your left. It will then be about thirty minutes over tundra and talus to the top. The summit is on the right (north) side of a ridge and has a small cairn. Some hand work will be necessary if you wish to traverse the ridge to the subpeak at the south end of the ridge. Descend via the first described route from the Buffalo Cabin by picking up the clear trail where the bushes begin below the summit talus and tundra.

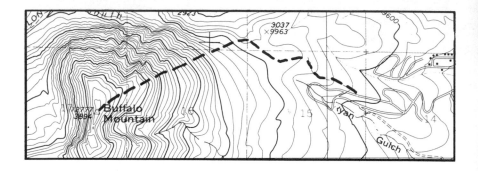

64. Peak 8 12,987 feet

Hike Distance: 4.4 miles each way
Hiking Time: Up in 160 minutes. Down in 115 minutes.
Starting Elevation: 11,000 feet
Elevation Gain: 2,187 feet (includes 100 feet of extra elevation gain each
                       way).
Difficulty: Moderate
Trail: From trailhead to the saddle between Peak 8 and Peak
                       9. (The Wheeler Trail.)
Relevant Maps: Breckenridge 7½ minute
                       Summit County Number Two
                       Arapaho National Forest
Views from the summit: N to Peak 7 through 1
                       E to Breckenridge
                       S to Peak 9
                       SE to Bald Mountain and Mount Guyot
                       SW to Jaque Peak
                       W to Copper Mountain

Comment:

The eastern slopes Peak 8 and 9 constitute the Breckenridge Ski Area. Breckenridge was named after President Buchanan's, Vice President, John Cabell Breckinridge of Kentucky. When he became a Confederate general, Union supporters in the area agitated to change the first I to an E.

The hike is mostly above timberline with great views to the east. From the top Copper Mountain, Breckenridge and Lake Dillon can all be seen.

Directions to the trailhead:

From Ski Hill Road in Breckenridge drive south on Colorado 9 for 2.2 miles and turn right onto Crown Road. Follow Crown Road for a half mile and take a right fork and join the Spruce Creek Road. Keep straight on the Spruce Creek Road past several side roads for 1.4 miles from the Crown Road fork and keep left at a fork and sign. (The right fork leads to Lower Crystal Lake.) Continue up the left fork for another half mile to a junction with the Wheeler Trail at a sign. Turn right (north) and ascend the road for two hundred and fifty yards and park on the left near a Wheeler Trail sign. Regular cars with good clearance can reach this point.

The Hike:

Head northwest on a trail and gradually up and over logs at Crystal Creek. Ascend a ridge continuing northwest and traverse the eastern flanks of Peaks 10 and 9 en route to a saddle between Peaks 8 and 9. The trail will continue west and north from this saddle down to Copper Mountain. However, leave the trail at the saddle and proceed north and up a ridge for 0.8 miles to a cairn at the summit. Descend via the same route. (From the Peak 8 summit it is only 0.45 miles north to the lower Peak 7 with no special danger or difficulty if you wish to extend your trip.)

Peak 8 from Breckenridge

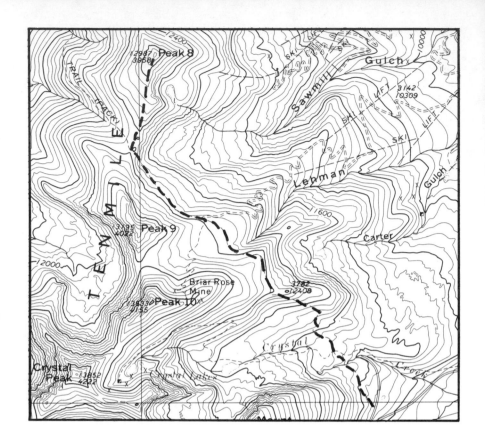

65. Matterhorn Peak 13,590 feet

Hike Distance: 4.5 miles each way
Hiking Time: Up in 143 minutes. Down in 103 minutes.
Starting Elevation: 10,390 feet
Elevation Gain: 3,200 feet
Difficulty: Moderate (some easy hand work is needed near the top).
Trail: Initial 3.6 miles and the final 0.2 miles
Relevant Maps: Uncompahgre Peak 7½ minute
                    Hinsdale County Number One
                    Uncompahgre National Forest
Views from the summit: NE to Uncompahgre Peak
                       SE to Broken Hill
                       SW to Wetterhorn Peak
                       WNW to Coxcomb Peak and Redcliff

Comment:

This hike requires less elevation gain, route finding, rock work and risk than
the adjacent Wetterhorn Peak. In naming Matterhorn and Wetterhorn Peaks

after their Swiss counterparts, their names seemingly should have been reversed since in Switzerland the Matterhorn is the higher and has the more dramatic summit while the Colorado Wetterhorn has these two characteristics when compared to the Colorado Matterhorn.

Directions to the trailhead:

From Colorado 149 in Lake City, drive west on Second Avenue just north of the Henson Creek Bridge. This road quickly turns left (south) and then follows Henson Creek to the west. It eventually leads over Engineer Pass to Ouray and Silverton but you will not go that far. Drive 9.3 miles from Colorado 149 to a fork at the old site of Capitol City. Turn right (northwest) up the North Fork of Henson Creek for 2.0 miles and park around Matterhorn Creek and a road leading north and up the creek. Regular cars can come this far but four wheel drive is required for the 0.7 miles north up Matterhorn Creek until the road is blocked.

The Hike:

Proceed up this rough road to the north which is marked by a sign, "Ridge Stock Driveway Trail." This road keeps to the right of Matterhorn Creek and is quite steep to above timberline. In half an hour you will reach the blockade of the road to vehicles and in another 30 minutes you pass a wilderness sign (The Big Blue Wilderness). Follow the road as it passes timberline and curves northeast away from the creek and then north again. Matterhorn Peak lies directly ahead. Do not confuse it with the taller Wetterhorn Peak to the left (south). When you can see a direct route up Matterhorn's southeast ridge without losing any elevation leave the road to your left and proceed northwest and up over steep tundra. When the tundra ends and the rocks begin, a trail emerges and continues up an easily negotiated couloir to the unmarked summit rock pile. Descend by your ascent route.

Matterhorn Peak from the southeast

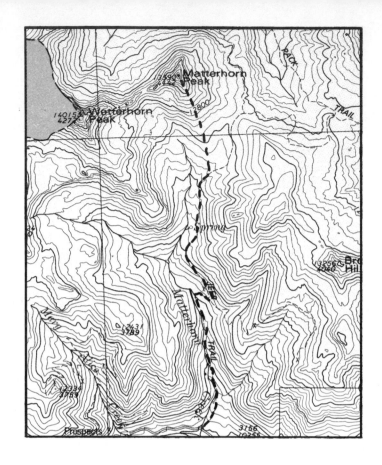

66. Bills Peak 12,703 feet

Hike Distance: 4.8 miles each way
Hiking Time: Up in 151 minutes. Down in 110 minutes.
Starting Elevation: 9,708 feet
Elevation Gain: 3,195 feet (includes 100 feet of extra elevation gain each
                    way)
Difficulty: Moderate
Trail: All the way until about 300 feet from the summit
Relevant Maps: Byers Peak 7½ minute
                    Ute Peak 7½ minute
                    Grand County Number Four
                    Arapaho National Forest
Views from the summit: N to Ptarmigan Peak (Grand County)
                    NNE to Fraser, Bottle Pass and Bottle Peak
                    NE to Byers Peak
                    ENE to Mount Flora
                    SSW to Peak 1, Tenmile Peak
                    and Ptarmigan Peak (Summit County)

Comment:

The trail for this hike is clear and exceptionally well marked. Horseshoe
Lake to the southwest of Bills Peak can readily be reached, is very pretty,
isolated with few visitors and worth the extra time and effort.

Directions to the trailhead:

From the Dillon and Silverthorne area at the intersection of Interstate 70
and Colorado 9, drive north on Colorado 9 for 12.8 miles. Then turn right
(east) on Summit County Road 15 also known as the Ute Pass Road. After
5.4 miles on this paved road you cross Ute Pass. In 2.2 more miles, take the
left fork and bypass the Henderson Mine. Keep left after 0.7 more miles and
in 0.9 more miles turn right at a sign onto Grand County Road 30. Follow
this good road for 2.6 miles and turn left (east) onto Grand County Road 302
and a sign directing you east to the Kinney Creek Trail. After 3.6 miles on
this road at a bend in the road just past Kinney Creek is the well marked
trailhead. Park here off the road.

The Hike:

Proceed east at the trail sign and register. Kinney Creek remains on your
right as you ascend the valley. In 50 minutes, you reach a fork and a sign.
The right fork leads to Horseshoe Lake in 2.5 miles. Take the left fork which
leads to Evalyn Lake and the St. Louis Divide Trail. In another 44 minutes,
you will arrive at a saddle and a sign having passed several poles in cairns.
The sign points left to the Keyser Ridge Road—2 miles and right to the
Keyser Creek Road—2 miles and to St. Louis Lake—4 miles. Turn right
(east) and follow the trail past timberline. At a ridge, turn right (south) and
pick up the trail which continues along the west side of the ridge. In about
54 minutes from the saddle, leave the trail at a cairn and ascend steeply
east to the Bills Peak summit which has an erroneous elevation sign in a
cairn. Return by your ascent route unless you wish to make a loop return by
way of Horseshoe Lake to the southwest. This will lengthen your day.

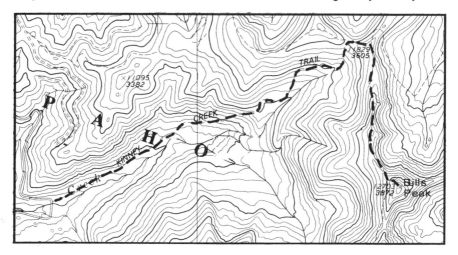

Bills Peak summit (left) from the north

Ptarmigan and Bottle Peaks from Bills Peak summit

67. Birthday Peak 12,730 feet

Hike Distance: 4.6 miles each way
Hiking Time: Up in 153 minutes. Down in 107 minutes.
Starting Elevation: 9,840 feet
Elevation Gain: 2,890 feet
Difficulty: Moderate
Trail: Initial 1.8 miles and intermittent thereafter
Relevant Maps: Mount Harvard 7½ minute
                  Mount Yale 7½ minute
                  Chaffee County Number Two
                  San Isabel National Forest
Views from the summit: N to Mount Harvard
                  NE to Mount Columbia
                  NW to Emerald Peak
                  E to Buena Vista
                  SE to Mount Yale
                  WNW to Ice Mountain

Comment:

This mountain forms part of the Continental Divide and lies on the boundary between Chaffee and Gunnison Counties. The trail which is used for the initial part of this hike, continues to Kroenke Lake, Browns Pass and over to the road from Buena Vista to Cottonwood Pass.

Directions to trailhead:

Drive north on U.S. 24 from the only stoplight in Buena Vista for 0.4 miles, or drive south on U.S. 24 from its intersection with Colorado 82 for 19.3 miles. Then turn west onto Crossman Avenue which is also Chaffee County Road 350. Drive 2.1 miles to a T and turn right on Chaffee County Road 361. After 0.9 miles, turn sharply left onto Chaffee County Road 365 at a sign, "North Cottonwood Creek 4 miles." Stay on this road for 5.3 miles as it goes west and up into the valley to a road end and a parking area. A sign alongside the trail reads: "North Cottonwood Creek Trail, Bear Lake 5 miles, Kroenke Lake 4 miles, Browns Pass 6 miles."

The Hike:

Proceed west up into the basin on the clear trail and cross two wooden bridges. About 1.8 miles from the trailhead, there is a fork. Keep left and continue toward Kroenke Lake. (The right turn goes to spectacular Horn Fork Basin at the foot of Mount Harvard and Mount Columbia.) After about 1.6 miles from the fork, you will reach a creek flowing toward the southeast. Just before this creek leave the main trail and hike northwest and up along the creek. A faint trail is present at first and intermittently as you ascend. It is 0.9 miles from the main trail to the saddle to the left of Birthday Peak and 0.3 miles more over tundra and talus to the top, which holds a small cairn and some scattered wooden poles and wire. Be sure to identify Birthday Peak to the northwest as you follow the creek to timberline. A slightly higher unnamed peak lies directly to the north as you arrive at timberline.

Birthday Peak from the southeast

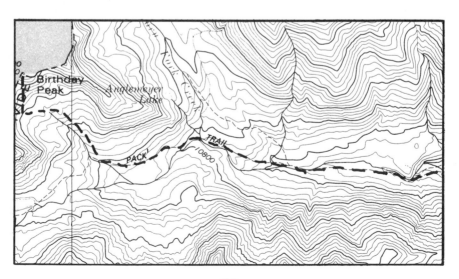

68. North Twin Cone Peak 12,319 feet and Mount Blaine 12,303 feet

Hike Distance: 4.5 miles each way
Hiking Time: Up to North Twin Cone Peak in 160 minutes. From North Twin Cone Peak to Mount Blaine in 32 minutes. Down in 130 minutes.
Starting Elevation: 10,050 feet
Elevation Gain: 2,422 feet
Difficulty: Moderate
Trail: All the way to the North Twin Cone summit
Relevant Maps: Jefferson 7½ minute
                 Mount Logan 7½ minute
                 Park County Number Two
                 Pike National Forest

Views from the summit: **From North Twin Cone Peak**
                 N to Mount Evans
                 E to Mount Blaine
                 SE to South Twin Cone Peak and McCurdy Mountain
                 W to Mount Guyot

                 From Mount Blaine
                 N to Mount Evans
                 S to South Twin Cone Peak
                 SE to McCurdy Mountain
                 W to North Twin Cone Peak and to Mount Guyot

Comment:

Kenosha Pass and Creek were named after the home town of a local stage coach driver, Kenosha, Wisconsin. By four wheel drive it is possible to reach the North Twin Cone Peak summit.

Directions to the trailhead:

Drive east from U.S. 285 at Kenosha Pass on the dirt road passing through a camping area. Take the right fork after entering the trees. After 1.0 mile from U.S. 285 you will encounter a metal gate which can be opened. Four-wheel drive can take you past this gate and even to the summit of North Twin Cone Peak. However, since regular passenger cars can reach this metal gate, the directions for this hike begin from the metal gate. Park off the road in this area.

The Hike:

Continue east on the road. Avoid the side roads which pass to the north and stay on the main road going east. In about one mile from the metal gate at the trailhead you pass through another unlocked gate. Shortly thereafter the road leaves Kenosha Creek and turns north (left) and becomes steeper with many curves and switchbacks. After about 90 minutes from the trailhead, you reach a place in the road with a blue diamond marker on a tree to the left and an arrow sign pointing straight ahead on the right. Take the faint mining road going left from the main road at this point. This faint road is soon blocked to larger vehicles. Continue on it as it passes north-east and upward passing a rocky formation on the left (west). Soon the trees become sparse and North Twin Cone Peak will be visible to the north-

123

east. Just before timberline, the faint road you are on joins the four wheel drive road going to the North Twin Cone Peak summit. You may continue on this road or leave the road and hike directly up to the top over the tundra.

At the summit is an old white box-like room with a collapsed metal antenna on its top. To reach Mount Blaine proceed east using the four wheel drive road briefly before heading directly to the collection of large boulders at the Mount Blaine summit. To descend, head southwest and regain the four wheel drive road and follow it to just below timberline where you pick up your ascent route.

South Twin Cone Peak from Mount Blaine

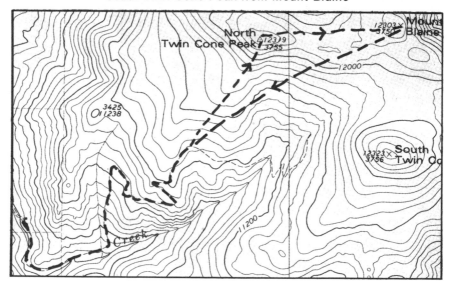

69. Republican Mountain 12,386 feet

Hike Distance: 5.6 miles each way
Hiking Time: Up in 157 minutes. Down in 106 minutes.
Starting Elevation: 9,000 feet
Elevation Gain: 3,506 feet (includes 60 extra feet each way)
Difficulty: Moderate
Trail: To just below timberline
Relevant Maps: Georgetown 7½ minute
                       Empire 7½ minute
                       Clear Creek County
                       Arapaho National Forest

Views from the summit: N to Parry Peak
                       NW to Colorado Mines Peak
                       E to Woodchuck Peak, Saxon Mountain and Griffith
                       Mountain
                       SSW to Mount Edwards, Grays Peak and Torreys
                       Peak
                       SE to Mount Evans and Mount Bierstadt
                       WNW to Robeson Peak and Engelmann Peak
                       WSW to Mount Sniktau

Comment:

Less than 50 miles from Denver the route up Republican Mountain should be free of snow between June and October. Four nearby "fourteeners" can be seen from the top.

Directions to the trailhead:

Drive south from Empire on the Bard Creek Road as it cuts off U.S. 40 in the center of town. Continue on this road for 2.0 miles as it curves west past Empire Pass overlooking Interstate 70 until you reach a rough road on your left. Park here. A regular car can come this far. Difficult four wheel driving would be required beyond this point toward Republican Mountain.

The Hike:

Start your hike to the south up the rough side road. After a few hundred yards take a left fork and stay on the main ascending road. After several curves in the road and passing several mining ruins, you will arrive at the high point of the road which is 4.5 miles from the trailhead. The top of Republican Mountain will now be visible ahead. The road continues down and east through Silver Gulch toward Georgetown. But you leave the road and its high point and angle up and west about a hundred yards through the sparse trees to the ridge. Then ascend west southwest along the ridge over the tundra to the rocky summit. Keep to the right of any residual snow. A benchmark and a pole mark the mountain top. Enjoy the sights before retracing the lengthy ascent route.

Republican Mountain from the east

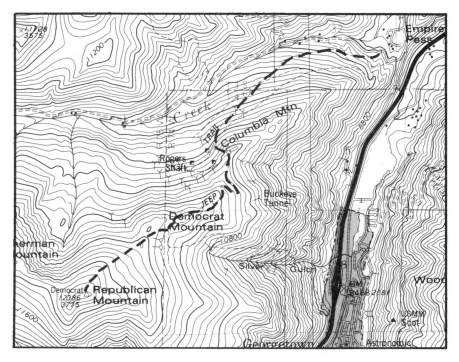

70. Paiute Peak 13,088 feet

Hike Distance: 4.0 miles each way
Hiking Time: Up in 165 minutes. Down in 125 minutes.
Starting Elevation: 10,470 feet
Elevation Gain: 2,718 feet (includes 50 feet of extra elevation gain each way).
Difficulty: Moderate
Trail: Initial 3 miles
Relevant Maps: Monarch Lake 7½ minute
Ward 7½ minute
Boulder County
Roosevelt National Forest
Views from the summit: N to Mount Meeker
NNW to Chiefs Head Peak, Pagoda Mountain and Longs Peak
ENE to Mount Audubon
SSE to Mount Toll, Navajo Peak and Apache Peak
SE to Kiowa Peak
W to Grand Lake

Comment:

The Paiute are tribes of American Indians who spend considerable energy digging up roots for food. This peak lies on the Continental Divide and the boundary between Grand and Boulder Counties and between the Roosevelt and Arapaho National Forests. The summit lies inconspicuously northwest of Blue Lake in the Indian Peaks Wilderness Area.

Directions to the trailhead:

From Nederland drive west and then north on Colorado 72 for about 11.7 miles. Turn left (west) onto the road to Brainerd Lake. After 4.9 miles on this road, keep left and cross two bridges at the edge of Brainerd Lake. Take right forks at 5.35 miles, at 5.5 miles and at 5.7 miles and park in the Mitchell Lake and Blue Lake lot at 5.85 miles from Colorado 72.

The Hike:

Take the trail leading west. It begins to the left of a wooden sign and map. Soon a bridge crosses a creek, later you will cross another creek over logs and Mitchell Lake is reached in about 18 minutes. Follow the clear trail for another 42 minutes to Blue Lake with Mount Toll looming impressively to the west. Continue on the trail as it curves to the right around the lake and continues upward to the west and ends near a smaller lake. Leave this lake and ascend to your right (northwest) over boulders to a higher lake. Keep left of this lake and continue up a moderately steep gulch to the northwest. The footing is loose at times as you ascend to a saddle and then north to a flat summit. A boulder with a pile of rocks and a makeshift register mark the high point. Avoid the temptation to descend to the east toward Mount Audubon (unless you wish to hike to its summit), and return more securely by your ascent route.

Mount Toll from the route up Paiute Peak

Longs Peak from the Paiute Peak summit

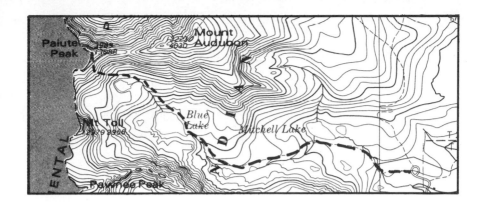

71. Ganley Mountain 12,902 feet and Pendleton Mountain 12,275 feet

Hike Distance: 4.3 miles to Ganley Mountain. 1.7 miles further to Pendleton Mountain. 5.5 miles from Pendleton Mountain to the Waldorf site.

Hiking Time: Up to Ganley Mountain in 145 minutes. To Pendleton Mountain in 40 minutes. Down in 140 minutes.

Starting Elevation: 11,594 feet

Elevation Gain: 1,808 feet (includes 500 feet of extra elevation gain on the return).

Difficulty: Moderate

Trail: Initial 80%

Relevant Maps: Grays Peak 7½ minute
Clear Creek County
Arapaho National Forest

Views from the summit: **From Ganley Mountain**
N to Breckinridge Peak and Sherman Mountain
NNE to Republican Mountain
NE to Pendleton Mountain, Griffith Mountain
and Alpine Peak
NNW to Silver Plume Mountain
NW to Woods Mountain, Mount Parnassus,
Bard Peak and Robeson Peak
E to Sugarloaf Peak
ESE to Gray Wolf Mountain, Mount Spalding,
Mount Evans and Mount Bierstadt
S to Mount Edwards
SE to Otter Mountain, Mount Wilcox and
Square Top Mountain
SW to Grays Peak, Torreys Peak, Kelso Mountain
and Grizzly Peak
W to Mount Sniktau and Mount Bethel

From Pendleton Mountain
N to Republican Mountain and Sherman Mountain
NW to Woods Mountain, Mount Parnassus,

Bard Peak and Robeson Peak
NNW to Silver Plume Mountain
NE to Griffith Mountain
E to Sugarloaf Peak
ESE to Gray Wolf Mountain, Mount Spalding
Mount Evans and Mount Bierstadt
S to Argentine Peak
SSE to Mount Wilcox and Square Top Mountain
SE to Otter Mountain
SW to Mount Edwards, Grays Peak, Torreys Peak
and Ganley Mountain
W to Mount Bethel
WNW to Hagar Mountain and Pettingell Peak
WSW to Mount Sniktau

Comment:

This hike is totally above timberline. Ganley Mountain is named for John W. Ganley, the first postmaster of Silver Plume, Colorado.

Pendleton Mountain was named after George H. Pendleton, the vice presidential running mate of General George McClellan on the unsuccessful Democratic ticket of 1864.

Directions to the trailhead:

From the intersection of Sixth and Rose Streets in Georgetown, drive south and up toward Guanella Pass for 2.8 miles to a dirt road on your right. Turn off onto this road and take right forks at 0.25 miles, 0.5 miles and also at 1.0 miles from the paved road. In 0.2 miles further take a sharp left fork and continue up the basin for a total of 6.25 miles from the paved road to an intersection of several roads at the old site of the Waldorf Mine. Regular cars can usually make it at least this far. Park here. (N.B. These directions utilize the better of two roads going southwest to the old Waldorf site. A lower road stays lower and close to Leavenworth Creek and requires four wheel drive.)

The Hike:

Begin up the road going north. After 0.65 miles, take the right fork and just beyond at a 4 way intersection continue straight (north). In 0.3 miles, take the right fork and a sharp left fork in 0.3 more miles. The road continues in switchbacks and in 0.6 miles take the right fork and again 0.1 miles later. In another 1.4 miles take the right fork and soon thereafter leave the road and ascend to the left (northwest) over tundra to the summit of Ganley Mountain. A small cairn lies at the top. The view southwest to Stevens Gulch and Grays and Torreys Peaks is especially rewarding.

Descend northeast and lose about 600 feet over the 1.7 miles of tundra to the top of Pendleton Mountain. Note that this peak is lower than the intervening high points. The summit is marked by a small cairn. Return to the road via the southwest and return to your car at the Waldorf site as you ascended. Be sure on your drive back down Leavenworth Gulch that you take the sharp right fork after 5.0 miles from Waldorf.

Grays Peak, Torreys Peak, Kelso Mountain and Grizzly Peak from Ganley Mountain.

Ganley Mountain from Interstate 70 west of Bakerville

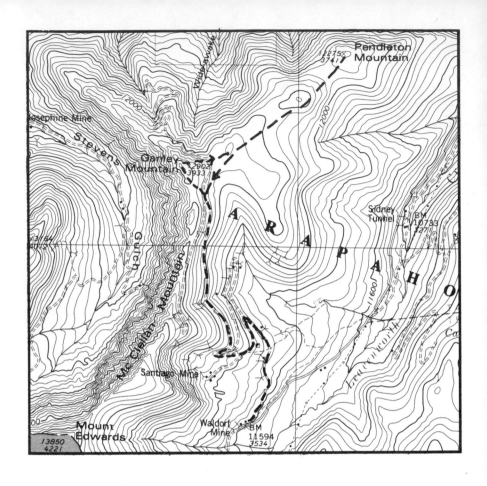

72. Grays Peak 14,270 feet and Torreys Peak 14,267 feet

Hike Distance: 4.3 miles from trailhead to Grays Peak. 0.7 miles from Grays Peak to Torreys Peak. 4.5 miles from Torreys Peak to trailhead. (Total 9.5 miles)

Hiking Time: Up to Grays Peak in 135 minutes. From Grays to Torreys in 35 minutes. From Torreys Peak summit to trailhead in 90 minutes.

Starting Elevation: 11,230 feet

Elevation Gain: 3,944 feet (includes 894 extra feet—mostly between summits)

Difficulty: Moderate

Trail: All the way

Relevant Maps: Grays Peak 7½ minute
Clear Creek County
Arapahoe National Forest

Views from the summit: **From Grays Peak**
N to Longs Peak and Mount Meeker
NNE to Kelso Mountain and Navajo Peak
NE to Chief Mountain, Ganley Mountain and McClellan Mountain
NW to Torreys Peak, Pettingell Peak, Mount Parnassus and Bard Peak
E to Mount Evans, Mount Spalding, Gray Wolf Mountain and Mount Wilcox
ENE to Mount Edwards and Otter Mountain
ESE to Mount Argentine, Square Top Mountain and Mount Bierstadt
SSE to Ruby Mountain
SSW to Santa Fe Peak, Mount Silverheels, Mount Guyot and Bald Mountain
SE to Pikes Peak
SW to Mount Democrat, Mount Lincoln, Quandary Peak, Pacific Peak, Dillon Reservoir, Mount of the Holy Cross, Peak 1 and Buffalo Mountain
WNW to Grizzly Peak and Chihuahua Lake
WSW to Lenawee Mountain

Views from the **Torreys Peak summit** are essentially the same as from Grays Peak except that Grays Peak is SE, Mount Sniktau is NW, Mount Parnassus and Bard Peak are NNW and Grizzly Peak is WSW.

Comment:

These peaks were named after the famous botanists, Asa Gray and John Torrey by Charles C. Parry. They are considered two of the easier fourteeners to climb in Colorado. These are very popular hikes due to their proximity to Denver. A herd of Rocky Mountain Goats are often present near the trail.

Directions to the trailhead:

Drive south from Interstate 70 at Bakerville (Exit 221) for 3.2 miles up Stevens Gulch to a trailhead parking lot on the left. En route stay on the wide, main, dirt road and keep left at mile 1.2 and at mile 2.3. Regular cars can reach the trailhead.

The Hike:

Begin southwest over the bridge. Follow the wide trail up past timberline with Mount Kelso above on the right. After a mile and a quarter from the trailhead, cross the creek. The top of Grays Peak is visible throughout the entire hike. Near the summit there are several connecting trails which lead to the top. The final thousand feet of elevation are over a talus trail to reach a rock shelter at the high point.

To continue over to Torreys Peak, descend northwest on a faint trail to the saddle. Then ascend the ridge over talus to a rock pile atop Torreys Peak. Enjoy the views and descend to the saddle and continue 50 feet up toward Grays Peak before turning left on the trail back to the Grays Peak Trail. This segment is snow-covered most of the hiking season.

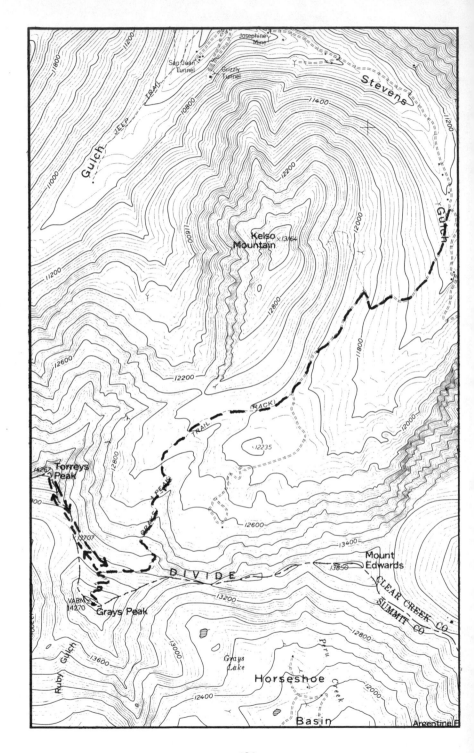

73. Rosedale Peak 11,825 feet

Hike Distance: 5.1 miles each way
Hiking Time: Up in 186 minutes. Down In 134 minutes.
Starting Elevation: 8,960 feet
Elevation Gain: 2,865 feet
Difficulty: Moderate
Trail: First 80% (to the unnamed pass).
Relevant Maps: Harris Park 7½ minute
                   Park County Number Two
                   Pike National Forest
Views from the summit: N to Chief Mountain and Squaw Mountain
                          E to Meridian Hill
                          SW to Mount Logan
                          W to Rosalie Peak
                          WNW to Mount Evans

Comment:

Rosedale Peak lies at the eastern edge of the so-called Pegmatite Points. The summit ridge forms part of the boundary between the Pike and the Arapaho National Forests.

Directions to the trailhead:

From U.S. 285 2.7 miles east of Bailey or 4.5 miles west of Pine Junction, turn north on Park County Road 43 and continue for 6.9 miles to a fork. Take the right turn which is Park County Road 47. After 1.0 miles further, a dirt road leads off left (north) and has a sign indicating that this road leads to the Meridian Campground and Camp Rosalie. This road is often blocked. Park nearby since this dirt road is the beginning of the trail.

The Hike:

Proceed north on the dirt road and pass the Meridian Campground on your left. At a fork go right and then left at the next two forks. A sign may be present directing you to the Meridian Trail. After about 18 minutes from the trailhead, another fork is reached. The left route is Church Fork Road. Take the right fork which is the Meridian Trail. Continue north on the trail and soon you reach a clearing and a horse corral on your left. A sign indicates that the road will dead end. A trail cuts off to the right, crosses Elk Creek by way of a small wooden bridge and then cuts left (north) and gradually ascends to reach an unnamed and unmarked pass at 10,700 feet. Continue north about 200 yards past the pass on the trail and then bushwhack left (west) and steeply up for 0.9 miles to a summit ridge and then to a summit boulder. Keep north on the ridge. The high point is on the west end of the ridge. There are no markers at the top. Descend by the ascent route.

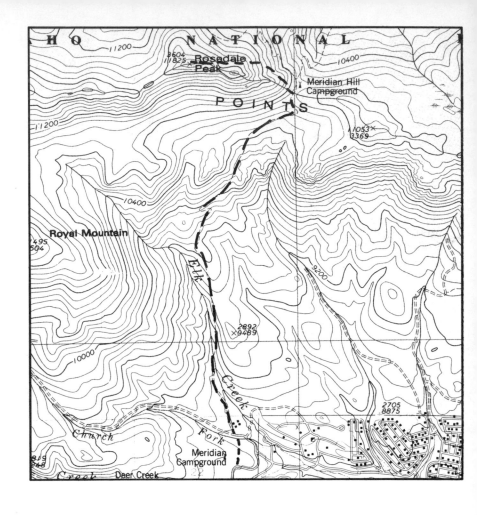

74. Breckinridge Peak 12,889 feet

Hike Distance: 5.1 miles each way
Hiking Time: Up in 165 minutes. Down in 110 minutes.
Starting Elevation: 9,800 feet
Elevation Gain: 3,419 feet (includes 165 feet of extra elevation gain each
                    way).
Difficulty: Moderate
Trail: About 80% of the way: from trailhead to the foot of the
                    peak.
Relevant Maps: Empire 7½ minute
                    Clear Creek County
                    Arapaho National Forest

Views from the summit: N to Witter Peak and Mount Eva

WNW to Mount Flora
S to Grays Peak and Torreys Peak
SSW to Cone Mountain
SW to Engelmann Peak and Red Mountain
SE to Mount Evans

Comment:

Named by E.H.N. Patterson on October 4, 1860, this is actually a subpeak of Mount Flora to the west. The Conqueror group of mines numbered over ten and were begun in 1881 to mine gold and silver. After closing down, they reopened again in 1901. The striking abandoned mine building north of the trailhead was part of this complex. The peak maintains the original spelling of President Buchanan's Vice President, John Cabell Breckinridge.

Directions to the trailhead:

From the center of Empire on U.S. 40 drive north on Main Street. Take right forks at 0.7, 1.1, 1.6, 1.8 and 1.9 miles. Stay on the main road, which requires no special vehicle, and park at mile 2.3 from U.S. 40 at the former Conqueror Mine.

The Hike:

Begin southwest on the road which becomes rougher. Stay on the main road and avoid side roads to the left at mile 0.1, 0.2 and 0.3. The road then curves left. Keep straight at a 4-way intersection at mile 0.6 and 100 yards farther go right. Take another right fork in 0.2 more miles and within 100 yards farther, take the first of five consecutive left forks over the next mile. The last of these leads steeply north northwest to a T. Go left and make a quick right fork and ascend to a ridge. Keep west on the ridge and take two more left forks before arriving at the foot of Breckinridge Peak. Leave the road and ascend west northwest up the ridge for another mile and a half to a cairn at the summit. Return by retracing your ascent route and be careful to take the correct trail forks.

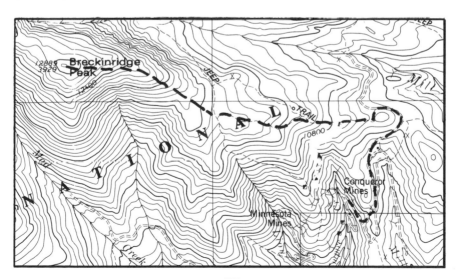

Breckinridge Peak from the southeast

75. Engelmann Peak 13,362 feet and Robeson Peak 13,140 feet

Hike Distance: Trailhead to Engelmann Peak summit—1.65 miles. Engelmann Peak summit to Robeson Peak summit—0.9 miles. Robeson Peak summit to trailhead—2.7 miles (loop).

Hiking Time: Up in 180 minutes. Down in 95 minutes.

Starting Elevation: 10,200 feet

Elevation Gain: 3,502 feet (includes 340 feet of extra elevation gain between the two peaks).

Difficulty: Moderate

Trail: Only over the final talus en route to the Engelmann summit and the final 1.75 miles of the descent route.

Relevant Maps: Berthoud Pass 7½ minute
                 Grays Peak 7½ minute
                 Clear Creek County
                 Arapaho National Forest

Views from the summit: **From Engelmann Peak**
                 NNW to Stanley Mountain and Vasquez Peak
                 NNE to Berthoud Pass and Colorado Mines Peak
                 NW to Red Mountain
                 S to Robeson Peak and Bard Peak
                 SE to Silver Plume Mountain
                 W to Woods Mountain and Citadel Peak (unofficial name)

138

From Robeson Peak:
Same as above except N to Engelmann Peak

Comment:

The higher peak is named after George Engelmann, a botanist and physician from St. Louis. The Engelmann Spruce is also named in his honor. The lower peak is named after the well known mining family of Georgetown. Solomon Robeson discovered many mines in Clear Creek County and his son, Jacob H. Robeson, was superintendent of the Dives Pelican Mine and mayor of Georgetown in 1898.

The hike is best done in September when the creek on your descent from the Engelmann-Robeson saddle will be at its lowest level.

Directions to the trailhead:

On U.S. 40 drive 7.4 miles west from Main Street in Empire toward Berthoud Pass or 5.9 miles south of Berthoud Pass. Turn left at the bend in the road and take the road marked toward the Henderson Mine. Pass the Big Bend Picnic Ground and after 0.4 miles from U.S. 40 take the left fork toward the old Urad Mine. This road becomes unpaved and after 0.9 miles from the fork park off the road at a spacious flat area.

The Hike:

Proceed due east over a grassy but rocky field above a tailings pond. Enter the trees and ascend steeply continuing to the east until you gain a ridge below timberline. Turn right (south) on this ridge and continue to ascend past timberline to another ridge from which the Engelmann summit becomes visible. This is all steep going but the footing is firm. Continue south over tundra to a talus slope which has a trail to the top of Engelmann Peak. A small cairn is the only marking. Continue south for a mile to Robeson Peak mostly over tundra. You will lose about 560 feet to the saddle and then ascend 340 feet to the flat unmarked top of Robeson Peak. To descend return to the Robeson-Engelmann saddle and then pass downward and west into a chute of scree and talus. A creek begins in this chute. Follow the creek to an abandoned mine below timberline. A trail begins here and continues west and north until it meets an old mining road running parallel to Ruby Creek. Turn right (north) onto this mining road until it ends at a locked fence. Pass around the fence and reach the Urad Mine road. In about a mile north on this road you will be back at your car.

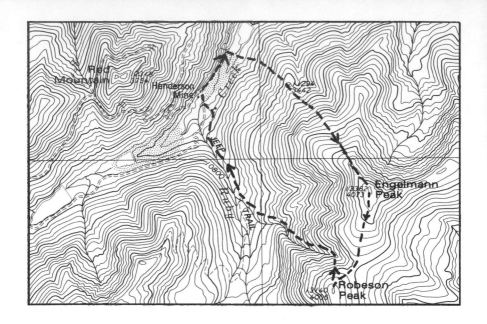

76. Bison Peak 12,431 feet

Hike Distance: 6.7 miles up and 4.1 miles down (loop).
Hiking Time: Up in 180 minutes. Down in 105 minutes.
Starting Elevation: 9,910 feet
Elevation Gain: 2,521 feet
Difficulty: Moderate
Trail: All the way until a few hundred feet below the summit.
                    Last two miles on the descent.
Relevant Maps: Farnum Peak 7½ minute
                    McCurdy Mountain 7½ minute
                    Topaz Mountain 7½ minute
                    Park County Number Two
                    Pike National Forest

Views from the summit: NNE to Windy Peak
                       NW to Mount Evans
                       W to Mount Guyot
                       S to Mount Silverheels
                       SE to McCurdy Mountain and to Pikes Peak

Comment:

Bison Peak is the highest in the Tarryall Range. The name Tarryall is said to have originated when miners found such abundant gold in this area that they believed there was enough for all (Tarry-all). McCurdy Mountain is an easy tundra walk of 2 miles to the southeast if you have the time and the energy.

Directions to the trailhead:

Drive on U.S. 285 for 3.2 miles south of the Kenosha Pass Campground and turn east onto a good dirt road marked by a sign, "Lost Creek Road." (This road lies just north of the town of Jefferson.) Stay on this main dirt road going ESE for 19.7 miles and park. Regular passenger cars should have no trouble getting this far.

The Hike:

To the south near the creek on the south side you will see some signs and a trail passing east-west. This trail has a south form passing up into the trees at a clearing and is the Indian Creek Trail — Number 607. Follow this trail south into Willow Gulch and eventually reach a large open valley. After about 4.7 miles, the Indian Creek Trail reaches Bison Pass at 11,100 feet. Here lies a three-way trail intersection. Signs direct you to Tarryall Creek 4 miles to the south, to Lost Creek 5¼ miles north (the route you have just taken) and McCurdy Park 5¾ miles to the east. Follow this McCurdy Park Trail up and to the east to above timberline where numerous, impressive red rock formations are encountered. As the trail turns south, leave it and head NE to Bison Peak and its clearly visible red, rocky summit. Avoid the labyrinth of boulders lying to the south of the peak and reach the unambiguous summit where the ruins of an old platform, a stone stove and a register jar can be found. For the descent hike northwest on the ridge tundra and pick your way down and bushwhack mostly to the northwest to regain the Indian Creek Trail in the large open valley visible below. Then continue north and retrace your ascent route back to your car.

Bison Peak summit (left) from the southwest

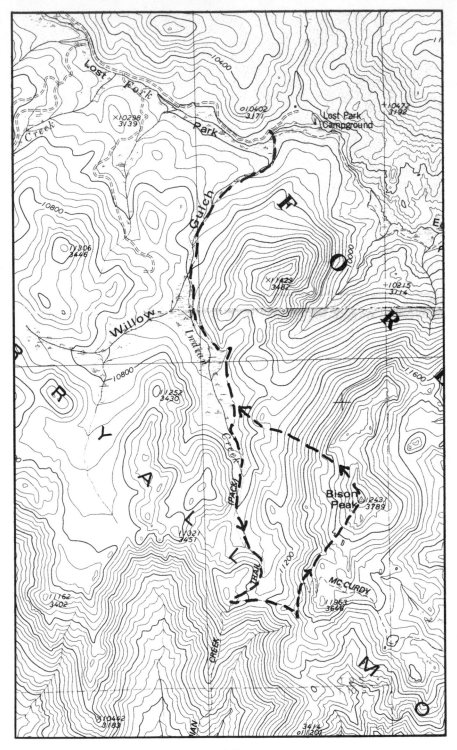

77. Corbett Peak 12,583 feet

Hike Distance: 4.8 miles on the ascent. 3.4 miles on the descent. (loop)
Hiking Time: Up in 190 minutes. Down in 100 minutes.
Starting Elevation: 9,560 feet
Elevation Gain: 3,023 feet
Difficulty: Moderate
Trail: Total below timberline. Intermittent above timberline.
Relevant Maps: Pando 7½ minute
                  Copper Mountain 7½ minute
                  Summit County Number Two
                  Eagle County Number Four
                  Arapaho National Forest
                  White River National Forest

Views from the summit: NE to Jaque Peak
                           NW to Elk Mountain
                           E to the Tenmile Range
                           S to North Sheep Mountain
                           W to Pearl Peak

Comment:

Kokomo Pass lies west of Kokomo Gulch and the now abandoned town of Kokomo. These places were named after Kokomo, Indiana, the home town of some of the area residents. Corbett Peak lies on the Elk Ridge which divides Eagle from Summit Counties.

Directions to the trailhead:

Drive on U.S. 24 either north from Leadville for 11.3 miles or south from Minturn for 18.8 miles. Turn northeast onto a dirt road. After 2.9 miles the road arrives at a T. Turn right for 0.7 more miles and park off the road. This point can be easily reached by regular passenger cars.

The Hike:

The trail begins on the north side of the road at a "No Motor Vehicles" sign. Continue north for about 180 yards to a fork and turn right (east) onto an old mining road which climbs rather steeply, crosses the Colorado Trail at an abandoned cabin, crosses Cataract Creek and generally proceeds to the east. At timberline, the creek is crossed again and the trail becomes intermittent to Kokomo Pass at 12,022 feet. The pass is the low point on the ridge to the east. From the unmarked pass follow the ridge trail north and then around to the northwest to gain the rocky outcroppings at the also unmarked top of Corbett Peak. Descend over the tundra to the southwest and rejoin the trail of your ascent route just below timberline and follow it west and southwest back to the trailhead.

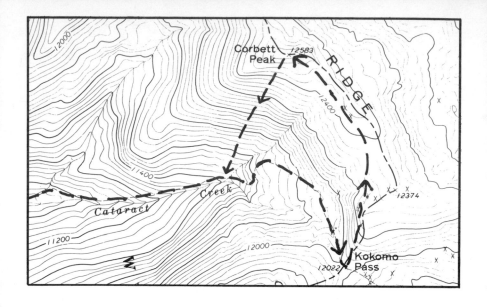

78. Long Scraggy Peak 8,812 feet

Hike Distance: 4.0 miles each way
Hiking Time: Up in 180 minutes. Down in 150 minutes.
Starting Elevation: 7,620 feet
Elevation Gain: 2,592 feet (includes 700 feet of extra elevation gain each way)
Difficulty: More difficult (some easy hand work necessary near the summit).
Trail: Intermittent.
Relevant Maps: Deckers 7½ minute
                  Platte Canyon 7½ minute
                  Jefferson County Number Two
                  Pike National Forest

Views from the summit: NW to Mount Evans
                  NNW to Raleigh Peak
                  ESE to Devils Head
                  S to Thunder Butte
                  SSW to Cheesman Mountain
                  SSE to Pikes Peak
                  WSW to Buffalo Peak, Windy Peak, Green Mountain and Little Scraggy Peak.

Comment:

Long Scraggy Peak looms like a battleship southeast of the town of Buffalo Creek. To reach the summit requires considerable bushwhacking and a compass. The area of this hike is traversed by many motorcycle trails which are heavily used on non-winter weekends. This hike should be free of snow between May and November.

Directions to the trailhead:

Drive south from U.S. 285 at Pine Junction on Jefferson County Road Number 126 for 12.1 miles to a dirt road on the left with a sign "Top of the World Campground 1.75 miles." Follow this road east and then as it curls southeast and then north. After 1.7 miles there is a fork. The right turn goes to the Top of the World Campground. Take the left fork for 0.6 more miles to a parking area on the right at a sign explaining the Raleigh Peak Multiple Use Soil and Water Project. Park here. Regular cars can drive this far.

The Hike:

Follow the trail heading southeast from the parking area. After about five minutes leave the trail and proceed to your right and directly toward Long Scraggy Peak which is visible in the distance. In another five minutes you reach the valley floor. Pick up an old mining road and turn left (east) and follow it along the creek. Various roads and motorcycle paths are present in the area. Continue east and east northeast and take the right fork at two consecutive trail intersections. It takes about 38 minutes and 700 feet of descent from the trailhead to reach the second right fork which now takes you on a trail south and up Spring Creek. Another fork is encountered in 12 minutes. Keep right again and head southeast. After about 20 minutes further on this trail leave it and Spring Creek and bushwhack left (southeast). Generally proceed southeast. At times old roads will assist you. Eventually as you ascend you will encounter an intermittent trail marked by red or white ribbons on the trees. These ribbons will lead you to the summit. Some easy hand work may be needed near the top. It will take about 110 minutes from when you leave Spring Creek to reach the top. At the rocky, open summit there is a wooden cross, a register cylinder and two U.S.G.S. markers. The best descent route is the same way you ascended. The drop-offs to the east and west are considerable.

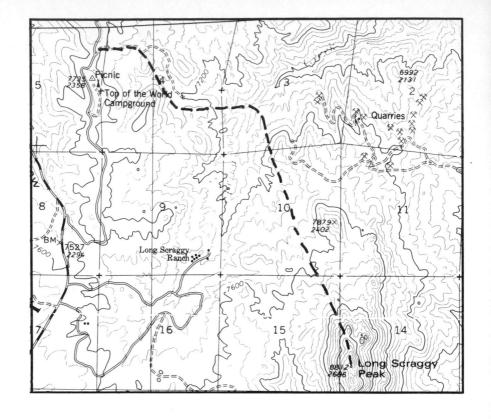

79. Mount Guyot 13,370 feet

Hike Distance: 4.75 miles on the ascent. 1.9 miles on the descent (loop)
Hiking Time: Up in 200 minutes. Down in 110 minutes.
Starting Elevation: 10,550 feet
Elevation Gain: 2,970 feet (includes 75 feet of extra elevation gain each
                    way).
Difficulty: More Difficult
Trail: All the way to French Pass and then along the ridge to
                    the top. Only on the final segment of the descent.
Relevant Maps: Boreas Pass 7½ minute
                    Summit County Number Two
                    Arapaho National Forest

Views from the summit: NE to Glacier Peak
                       E to Georgia Pass
                       SSW to Boreas Mountain
                       SW to Bald Mountain
                       W to Tenmile Range

146

Comment:

This peak is named after the Swiss surveyor, Professor Arnold Henry Guyot. The summit of Mount Guyot and French Pass also form part of the Continental Divide, the boundary between Summit and Park Counties and also between the Arapaho and Pike National Forests. Mount Guyot can be climbed more easily from Georgia Pass on the east.

Directions to the trailhead:

Drive 0.8 miles north from the stop light in Breckenridge (Lincoln Street) on Colorado 9. Turn right (east) onto Summit County Road 450 and drive generally south up French Gulch for 5.15 miles to a fork. The left fork leads up Little French Gulch and ends in 1.5 miles. Your hiking route will be the right fork and since the road can be rather rough beyond this point, park in this area. En route to this parking spot from Colorado 9 keep right at mile 0.4, left at mile 1.1, straight at mile 3.9, left at mile 4.0, left at mile 4.55 and at mile 4.65 you will drive through an open gate. Regular cars should be able to drive the 5.15 miles to the Little French Gulch cutoff.

The Hike:

Proceed on foot south and up French Gulch. In 1.8 miles you will reach a meaningless fork as both roads quickly converge at a locked, metal gate. Pass around the gate and cross the creek within one hundred yards. It is 2.2 miles further, mostly over tundra to French Pass which is marked by a cairn. Bald Mountain is on your right (west) and Boreas Mountain lies impressively straight ahead (south). Turn left and ascend to the east northeast and gain a trail leading north along the western side of the ridge. This trail eventually turns to the northeast to gain the cairn-marked summit. A register cylinder and some rock shelters are also at the top. Descend over talus to the northwest to a ridge which separates French Gulch from Little French Gulch. Around timberline veer to your left (northwest) and bushwhack down to the road which leads to your vehicle.

Mount Guyot from the south

147

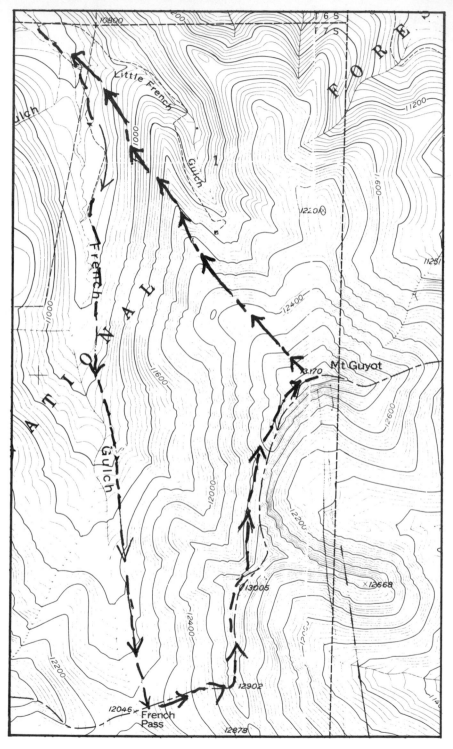

80. Satanta Peak 11,979 feet and Mount Neva 12,814 feet

Hike Distance:	2.8 miles to Arapaho Pass. 1.3 miles from Arapaho Pass to Satanta Peak. 1.25 miles from Arapaho Pass to Mount Neva.
Hiking Time:	Trailhead to Arapaho Pass in 93 minutes. Arapaho Pass to Satanta Peak in 26 minutes. Satanta Peak back to Arapaho Pass in 26 minutes. Arapaho Pass to Mount Neva in 88 minutes. Mount Neva back to trailhead in 130 minutes.
Starting Elevation:	10,180 feet
Elevation Gain:	Trailhead to Satanta Peak 2,049 feet (includes 125 feet of extra elevation gain each way). Trailhead to Mount Neva 2,834 feet (includes 100 feet of extra elevation gain each way). For both peaks 3,157 feet.
Difficulty:	More Difficult
Trail:	All the way except on the final ridges to Satanta Peak and to Mount Neva.
Relevant Maps:	East Portal 7½ minute
	Monarch Lake 7½ minute
	Boulder, County
	Grand County Number Four
	Arapaho National Forest
	Roosevelt National Forest

Views from the summit: **From Satanta Peak**
N to Mount Achonee
NNE to Lone Eagle Peak
NE to Apache Peak and Navajo Peak
E to North Arapaho Peak
ESE to Caribou Lake
SSE to Mount Neva
W to Meadow Creek Reservoir

From Mount Neva
N to Mount Achonee and Lake Dorothy
NNE to Lone Eagle Peak
NE to Apache Peak, Navajo Peak and
North Arapaho Peak
NW to Lake Granby
SW to Byers Peak

Comment:

Arapaho Pass and Mount Neva are on the Continental Divide and the boundary between Grand and Boulder Counties and the Roosevelt and Arapaho National Forests. This hike lies in the heavily used Indian Peaks Wilderness Area.

Directions to the trailhead:

From the junction of Colorado 72 and Colorado 119 in Nederland, drive south on Colorado 119 for 0.65 miles and turn right (west). Drive a total of 9.1 miles from Colorado 119 on this road through the town of Eldora to a parking area at the trailhead at the Fourth of July Campground. En route keep right at 1.5 miles and at 4.9 miles. Keep left at 7.7 miles and right to the parking area at 9.0 miles.

The Hike:

Proceed north and then west from the clearly marked trailhead. Take a right fork after 27 minutes (the left fork goes to Diamond Lake) and a left fork after 24 more minutes (the right fork goes to the Arapaho Glacier and the Arapaho Peaks). Continue west above timberline on the excellent trail, which now consists of mostly talus, to Arapaho Pass just east of Lake Dorothy. For Satanta Peak, continue west down from Arapaho Pass. The trail becomes a bit narrow at times but is adequate. In 13 minutes the trail brings you to a sign marking Caribou Pass. A trail leads northwest from the pass and the Caribou Pass Trail. Follow this trail for only a few hundred feet and then leave the trail and ascend north over tundra to a large cairn atop Satanta Peak. Return to Arapaho Pass by the same route. For Mount Neva continue west up the ridge on a faint trail from the area of Arapaho Pass. Follow the ridge as it turns south. At a few points along this ridge some moderate hand work is necessary. Continue south. You eventually reach a grassy area leading to a cairn at the summit. Return to Arapaho Pass and the trailhead by your ascent route. (An alternate descent route from Mount Neva is to go south along the ridge to a saddle and then to descend east into the basin toward Diamond Lake where you gain a trail leading east into the Arapaho Pass Trail on which you ascended.)

Satanta Peak (left) from Arapaho Pass

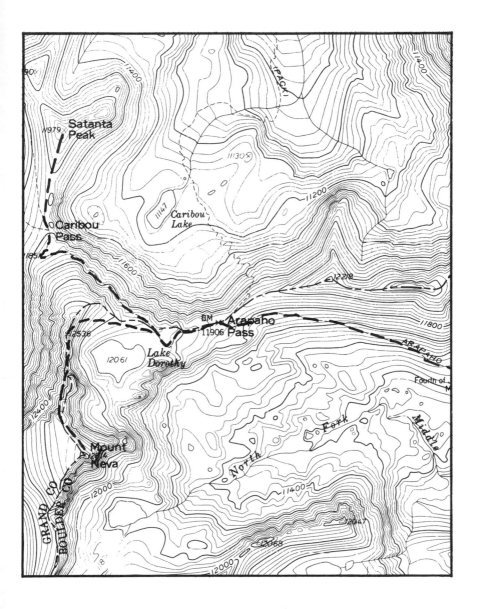

81. Mount Buckskin 13,370 feet

Hike Distance: 4.5 miles each way
Hiking Time: Up in 190 minutes. Down in 135 minutes.
Starting Elevation: 9,600 feet
Elevation Gain: 4,170 feet (includes 200 feet of extra elevation gain each
                    way).
Difficulty: More Difficult (some easy hand work may be needed
                    near the top).
Trail: All the way to Buckskin Pass. (3.7 miles).
Relevant Maps: Maroon Bells 7½ minute.
                    Pitkin County Number One
                    White River National Forest

Views from the summit: NW to Capitol Peak
                       E to Willow Lake
                       S to Buckskin Pass
                       SSE to North Maroon Peak
                       SE to Pyramid Peak and Willow Pass
                       SW to Snowmass Mountain
                       WSW to Snowmass Lake

Comment:

The Maroon Lake area is one of the most heavily used in Colorado. The
Maroon Creek Road is closed to private motor vehicles from 9:00 A.M. until
5:00 P.M. daily during the hiking season. Busses transport visitors from a
parking area at the mouth of the valley for the nine miles to Maroon Lake.
This hike brings you to one of the most scenic passes in Colorado and to a
summit which poses no special risks but which offers spectacular vistas.

Directions to the trailhead:

Drive west on Colorado 82 from Aspen. Cross the Castle Creek bridge and
take the first left turn after the stop light. This left turn directs you to Aspen
Highlands. After 0.1 miles on this road, take the right fork to Maroon Creek.
Follow this paved road up the valley for a total of 9.9 miles from Colorado 82
until the road ends at a parking area at Maroon Lake above the Maroon
Lake Campground. (Or you may prefer to pay for the public shuttle bus.)

The Hike:

Take the trail which begins at the west end of the parking area at a sign,
"Maroon Snowmass Trail Number 1975". This leads south and then turns
southwest before the lake. Take two right forks en route to a sign and trail
fork near Crater Lake. This fork will be reached in about 45 minutes. Take
the right fork and ascend southwest into Minnehaha Gulch. In about thirty
minutes from the Crater Lake fork take the right fork and in forty more
minutes reach timberline. About ten minutes above timberline take the left
fork at a sign. (The right fork goes to Willow Pass.) In another thirty minutes,
you will arrive after a series of switchbacks at unmarked but very scenic
Buckskin Pass. From the pass, proceed north over tundra. The Mount
Buckskin summit is visible 0.8 miles from the pass. En route you will lose
about one hundred feet of elevation as you reach a saddle. Continue north
and eventually over some rocky false summits to the top which has a cairn,
U.S.G.S. marker and a small register jar. Take the ascent route back to the
trailhead.

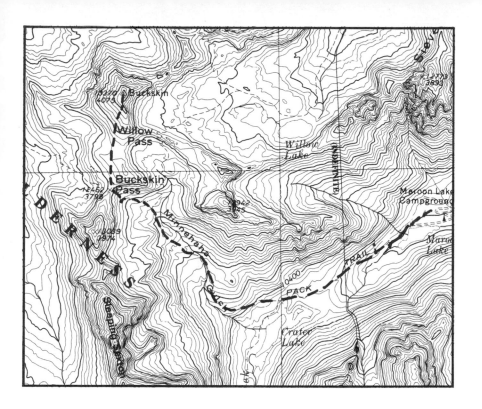

82. Uneva Peak 12,522 feet

Hike Distance: 6.5 miles to the summit. 5.5 miles down (loop).
Hiking Time: Up in 210 minutes. Down in 160 minutes.
Starting Elevation: 9,711 feet
Elevation Gain: 2,811 feet
Difficulty: More Difficult
Trail: Initial two-thirds
Relevant Maps: Vail Pass 7½ minute
                     Summit County Number Two
                     Arapaho National Forest - Dillon Ranger District

Views from the summit: N to Red Peak
                       NE to Buffalo Mountain
                       S to Jaque Peak
                       SSE to Copper Mountain
                       SW to Vail Pass
                       E to Peak 1

Comment:

Uneva Peak in the Gore Range lies on the boundary between Eagle and
Summit Counties. Uneva Lake is located east of the peak and out of contact

with this hiking route. It was an early recreational area for the residents of Frisco. The Wheeler Lakes are named after Judge John S. Wheeler, a South Park rancher who grazed his cattle in this area.

Directions to the trailhead:

Drive to a parking area just north of the junction of Interstate 70 with Colorado 91 near Copper Mountain. Park in this area which lies off of the east side of I-70 or nearby. More parking is available just east of Interstate 70 as it intersects Colorado 91.

The Hike:

Proceed southwest on a trail which begins just north of the bridge crossing Interstate 70 at Colorado 91. The trail quickly ascends to the northwest across from the Copper Mountain Ski Area. Keep left at a fork in the trail as the right fork leads to the Wheeler Lakes and ends there. The clear trail progresses west and then curves north to reach Uneva Pass at 11,900 feet. Uneva Peak will now be visible to the northwest at the end of a cirque. Proceed west to gain the ridge and then turn north to the summit which is marked by an U.S.G.S. marker and two nearby cairns. The best descent route passes directly to the south southeast over a grassy ridge. At the final subpeak of this ridge pass to the left and soon thereafter regain the trail you used on the ascent.

Uneva Peak (far right) from Uneva Pass

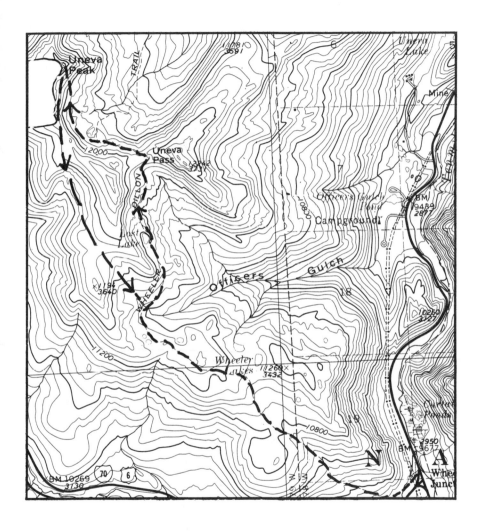

83. Bandit Peak   12,444 feet

Hike Distance: 5.0 miles up. 3.2 miles down (loop).
Hiking Time: Up in 214 minutes. Down in 122 minutes.
Starting Elevation: 9,248 feet
Elevation Gain: 3,246 feet (includes 50 feet lost just past the trailhead).
Difficulty: More Difficult
Trail: To the Pegmatite Points on the ascent and the last 2 miles of the descent.
Relevant Maps: Harris Park 7½ minute
                    Park County Number Two
                    Pike National Forest
Views from the summit: N to Rosalie Peak
                    NW to Epaulet Mountain
                    ENE to Rosedale Peak
                    E to Kataka Mountain
                    SW to Mount Logan

Comment:

Bandit is a subpeak of Rosalie Peak in the Mount Evans region of the Front Range. The Pegmatite Points are a series of rocky projections named for their coarse variety of granite, sometimes called graphic granite.

Directions to the trailhead:

From U.S. 285, 2.7 miles northeast of Bailey or 4.5 miles southwest of Pine Junction, drive north and then northwest on Park County 43 for 8.3 miles to Deer Creek Campground and then 0.8 miles further to a parking area and a trail sign nearby. Park here. (En route to this trailhead take the left fork after 7.0 miles and the right fork after 1.3 miles further.)

The Hike:

Take the trail to the right labeled the "Tanglewood Trail." (The trail to the left is the Rosalie Trail Number 603 and ultimately reaches Guanella Pass.) Lose a little altitude and continue northwest along Tanglewood Creek and keep right at a fork one mile from the trailhead. After 2.25 miles the trail reaches a pass with Rosalie Peak on your left and several rocky knobs, the Pegmatite Points, to your right. (The trail continues north and down to the Roosevelt Lakes and the Beartrack Lakes.) Leave the pass and the trail by going to the west (left) and south around a cirque for about 1.5 miles to the north ridge of Bandit Peak and ascend to the south easily from there to the cairn at the top. Descend by continuing south over tundra and through the trees to meet the Rosalie Trail which parallels Deer Creek. This will require about 60 minutes. Then turn left (east) onto this trail and it is about 2 miles and another hour to complete the loop back to the trailhead.

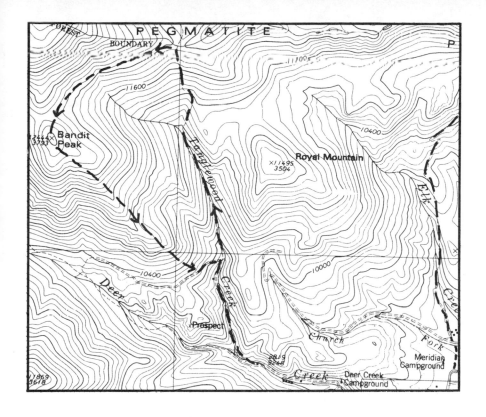

84. Kataka Mountain 12,441 feet

Hike Distance: 5.7 miles on the ascent. 3.6 miles on the descent. (loop)
Hiking Time: Up in 250 minutes. Down in 122 minutes.
Starting Elevation: 9,610 feet
Elevation Gain: 2,831 feet
Difficulty: More Difficult
Trail: For 4.5 miles on the ascent until 11,400 feet and for the
                     last 2.1 miles on the descent.
Relevant Maps: Mount Evans 7½ minute
                     Park County Number Two
                     Pike National Forest

Views from the summit: N to Mount Evans
                       NE to Bandit Peak
                       NNW to Mount Bierstadt
                       NW to Geneva Mountain
                       ESE to Mount Logan
                       SSW to South Park and the East and West
                       Buffalo Peaks
                       SW to Mount Guyot
                       WNW to Square Top Mountain

Comment:

Kataka is a discrete Park County summit which affords vistas of many peaks and of considerable distances. Park County was named after South Park and was one of the original territorial counties of Colorado.

Directions to the trailhead:

Either drive north from U.S. 285 at Grant on Park County Road 62 on the east side of Geneva Creek for 5.3 miles or south from Guanella Pass on Park County Road 62 for 8.1 miles to a parking area on the east side of the road. (Geneva Park is the name given the meadow on the west side of the road.) Park here.

The Hike:

The trailhead is well marked past an open wooden fence by a sign indicating that the Rosalie Trail intersection is 4 miles and that Abyss Lake is 8 miles. Since this is part of the Mount Evans Wilderness Area, the trail is closed to motorized vehicles but open to horseback travel. Hike northeast on this trail which parallels Scott Gomer Creek. After 2.1 miles from the trailhead the trail crosses the creek at a wooden bridge. In another 20 minutes the trail crosses the creek again back to its west side. After about two hours from the trailhead you reach a basin and a confluence of Scott Gomer Creek, coming from the northwest and the Lake Fork, coming from the northeast. Cross Scott Gomer Creek around the confluence and very quickly the trail reaches a fork. The left fork continues northeast to Abyss Lake. The right fork is the one you will take. It goes to Deer Creek and is called the Rosalie Trail. Continue east on this trail which rises to timberline after crossing the Lake Fork. When you are at about 11,400 feet, (just below timberline) and a subpeak of Mount Bierstadt lies directly to your north, leave the trail and proceed up and south over tundra and past sparse trees. A ridge below the Kataka summit lies to your south. It is about 1.2 miles from the trail, over this ridge to a small pile of rocks on the flat summit. For the return make a loop by proceeding due west and downward to regain the trail around the southernmost bridge which crosses Scott Gomer Creek. The trail then takes you southwest to the trailhead.

Mount Logan from Kataka Mountain summit

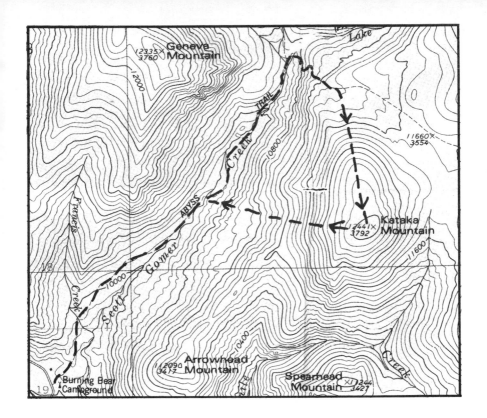

85. Comanche Peak 13,277 feet

Hike Distance: 5.4 miles each way
Hiking Time: Up in 214 mlnutes. Down in 142 minutes.
Starting Elevation: 8,940 feet
Elevation Gain: 4,337 feet
Difficulty: More Difficult
Trail: All the way
Relevant Maps: Horn Peak 7½ minute
                    Custer County Number One
                    Saguache County Number Five
                    San Isabel National Forest

Views from the summit: NE to Comanche Lake and Westcliffe
                       NW to Venable Peak
                       ESE to Horn Peak
                       SE to Humboldt Peak, Mount Adams and
                       Kit Carson Peak
                       SSE to Fluted Peak

Comment:

Westcliffe, the county seat of Custer County, lies in the Wet Mountain
Valley and overlooks the Sangre de Cristo Mountains to the west. Formerly

called Clifton, the town was renamed by Dr. W. A. Bell after his home town of Westcliff-on-the-Sea, England.

Directions to the trailhead:

Drive south from Westcliffe on Colorado Road 69 from its junction with Colorado 96 for 3.45 miles. Turn right onto County Road 140 and drive for 4.65 more miles to a T. Turn left onto County Road 141. After 0.75 miles on this road, take the left fork to Alvarado Campground. In 1.45 more miles take the left fork to a parking area at the Comanche Lake trailhead at the end of the road. Park here.

The Hike:

A sign at the southwest corner of the parking area directs you onto the clear Comanche Lake Trail. The first part of the trail has been cemented to prevent erosion. In about 11 minutes you will intersect the Rainbow Trail. Turn right and in 13 more minutes turn left at a sign directing you to "Comanche Lake 3.5 miles." Follow this trail as it curves west up the valley. Eventually Horn Peak becomes visible on your left across the valley. In about 114 minutes from the Rainbow Trail you will arrive at a point overlooking Comanche Lake with Comanche Peak looming impressively beyond at the end of the basin. Continue on the trail as it rises to the right of the lake in a series of switchbacks to reach an unnamed pass at 12,750 feet in about 53 minutes from Comanche Lake. Descend about forty feet from the pass to a saddle on your left. From here take the faint ridge trail up to the south over tundra to the Comanche Peak summit and a small cairn. It takes about 23 minutes from the saddle. Descend as you came up. (If you wish to prolong your outing and see a different valley on your return, take the trail north to an unnamed pass and then descend to the east over the so-called Phantom Terrace past the Venable Lakes to eventually reach the Rainbow Trail and eventually your car at the Alvarado Campground parking area. This loop will add about 30 minutes to your hike and 100 feet of elevation gain which is necessary to reach the second pass.) (cf Venable Peak.)

West toward Comanche Peak

Comanche Peak and Lake

North from Comanche Peak

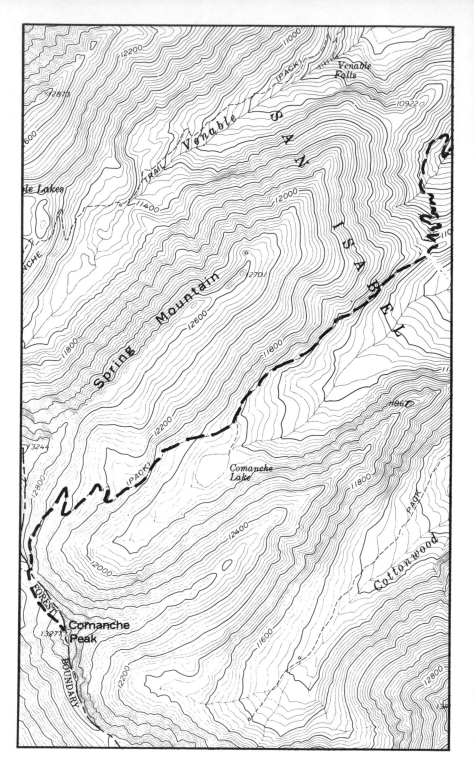

86. Venable Peak 13,334 feet

Hike Distance: 6.8 miles each way
Hiking Time: Up in 205 minutes. Down in 140 minutes.
Starting Elevation: 8,930 feet
Elevation Gain: 4,404 feet
Difficulty: More Difficult
Trail: All the way to the pass at 12,800 feet.
Relevant Maps: Horn Peak 7½ minute
Rito Alto Peak 7½ minute
Saguache County Number Five
Custer County Number One
Rio Grande National Forest
San Isabel National Forest
Views from the summit: N to the Wet Mountain Valley
NW to Eureka Mountain
ESE to Horn Peak and Spring Mountain
S to the San Luis Valley
SE to Comanche Peak, Fluted Peak, Humboldt
Peak, Crestone Needle, Mount Adams and Kit
Carson Peak.

Comment:

Part of this hike utilizes the Rainbow Trail, a 55 mile route along the eastern side of the Sangre de Cristo Mountain Range. The Abbot's Lodge which is passed early in the hike was owned and operated by the Benedictine Order for many years as a summer camp and as a support structure for the Holy Cross Abbey, a high school for boys in Canon City, Colorado. Venable Pass is not traversed in this route. It lies to the west of the Venable Lakes.

Directions to the trailhead:

Drive south from Westcliffe on Colorado 69 from its junction with Colorado 96 for 3.45 miles. Turn right onto Road 140 and continue for 4.65 miles to a T. Turn left here onto Road 141. After 0.75 miles on this road take the left fork to Alvarado Campground. In 1.45 miles a sign directs you up a right fork to the Venable Lake Trailhead. Park at the loop at the end of this road.

The Hike:

Follow the trail northwest from the parking area past the old Abbot's Lodge for less than a mile to join the Rainbow Trail. Turn right onto the Rainbow Trail and after 200 yards, take the left fork at a sign, "Venable Lakes 5 miles." Continue southwest up the valley with Venable Creek on your left. (A short side trail goes off left to Venable Falls.) Continue up on the main trail until it forks at an abandoned cabin. Take the left fork which leads to one of the Venable Lakes and soon thereafter to a fork with a sign. Take the left fork and rise southwest toward the unnamed pass by way of a narrow shelf with steep drop-offs. This part of the trail is known as the Phantom Terrace. At the pass there is no sign. Leave the trail here and ascend the ridge to the northwest and then curve south on the ridge to the summit cairn. Descend as you came up unless at the pass you wish to continue west on the trail and loop back to the Rainbow Trail as the trail curves south to the foot of Comanche Peak and then southeast and down past Comanche Lake to the Rainbow Trail.

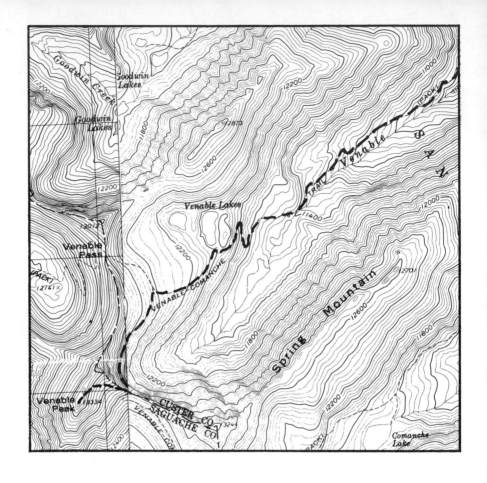

87. Mount Logan 12,871 feet

Hike Distance: 9.2 miles on the ascent and 4.55 miles for the descent. (loop)
Hiking Time: Up in 240 minutes. Down in 130 minutes.
Starting Elevation: 9,320 feet
Elevation Gain: 3,795 feet (includes 244 feet lost going over a subpeak on the ascent)
Difficulty: More Difficult (due to elevation gain and distance but no special risks)
Trail: On the ascent all the way until about one mile from the summit. On the descent for only the final two miles.
Relevant Maps: Harris Park 7½ minute
Mount Evans 7½ minute
Mount Logan 7½ minute
Park County Number Two
Pike National Forest

Views from the summit: N to Mount Bierstadt and Mount Evans
NE to Rosalie Peak, Bandit Peak and
Epaulet Mountain
NW to Kataka Mountain and Square Top Mountain
ENE to Rosedale Peak and Meridian Hill
S to Mount Blaine, North Twin Cone Peak and
South Twin Cone Peak
SE to Pikes Peak
WNW to Spearhead Mountain

Comment:

Mount Logan, like the Colorado county of the same name, was named after John Alexander Logan, an Illinois politician and a Union General in the Civil War. He inaugerated the national holiday of Memorial Day.

Directions to the trailhead:

Drive on U.S. 285 either 4.5 miles southwest from Pine Junction or 2.7 miles northeast from Bailey to Park County Road Number 43 which goes north and is paved. Follow this road (which eventually becomes unpaved but is passable by regular cars) for 9.1 miles to the Deer Creek Trailhead and road end. (En route to this trailhead take the left fork after 7.0 miles and after 1.3 miles further take the right fork at the Deer Creek Campground. It is then 0.8 miles more to the trailhead parking area.)

The Hike:

Go west a few hundred yards to trail signs and a fork. Take the left fork which is the Rosalie Trail. Follow this trail west and northwest along Deer Creek which you will cross several times for 5.8 miles to a ridge and a junction with the Threemile Creek Trail, Number 635. Follow the Threemile Creek Trail as it curves south and upward between Kataka Mountain on your right (west) and subpeaks of Mount Logan on your left (east). The trail becomes rather faint. Leave the trail, go southeast and hike up the subpeak of Mount Logan keeping to the right of its high point. At the ridge the true summit becomes visible to the south. Continue over tundra and lose 244 feet as you go directly toward the high point. From the Threemile Creek cutoff from the Rosalie Trail it is 3.1 miles to the top of Mount Logan which has a large ring of rocks, some old wooden planks and a register cylinder. To descend, hike over the tundra and rocks to the northeast. At the most easterly subpeak enter the trees and bushwhack through a moderately dense forest keeping northeast to regain the Rosalie Trail. A creek becomes evident after you enter the trees. Keep this creek to your left and follow it to its junction with Deer Creek and the trail. It is then 2 miles east to your car. (If you dislike bushwhacking, descend the same way you came up. This will add 4.65 miles to the hike.)

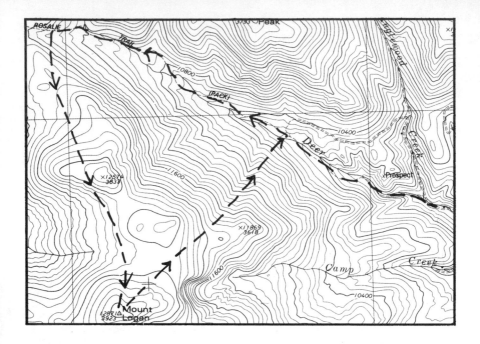

88. Buckeye Peak 12,867 feet and Mount Zion 12,126 feet

Hike Distance: 4.3 miles to Mount Zion. 3.1 miles further to Buckeye Peak. (7.4 miles each way.)
Hiking Time: Up in 220 minutes. Down in 180 minutes.
Starting Elevation: 9,961 feet
Elevation Gain: 3,426 feet (includes 260 feet of extra elevation gain each way).
Difficulty: More Difficult
Trail: Initial 90%
Relevant Maps: Leadville North 7½ minute
Lake County
San Isabel National Forest

Views from the summit: **From Buckeye Peak**
N to Jaque Peak
NE to Bartlett Mountain
NW to Cooper Hill
ENE to Mount Lincoln, Mount Cameron and Mount Democrat
ESE to Mount Arkansas
S to La Plata Peak, Leadville and Mount Zion
SE to Mosquito Peak and Mount Sherman
SSE to Mount Princeton, Mount Yale, Mount Columbia, Mount Harvard and Mount Belford
SW to Mount Elbert, Turquoise Lake, Mount Massive, Galena Mountain, Pyramid Peak, North and South Maroon Peaks, Snowmass Mountain and Capitol Peak
WNW to Mount of the Holy Cross

166

The views from **Mount Zion** are essentially the same with Buckeye Peak to the north.

Comment:

Buckeye Peak was probably named by some early miners from Ohio, the Buckeye State. A buckeye is a type of tree with distinctive markings. There are several Mount Zions in Colorado. The vistas from both summits are exceptional with at least eighteen fourteeners visible.

Directions to the trailhead:

From the north end of Leadville at the intersection of Colorado 91 and U.S. 24 drive northwest on U.S. 24 for 1.4 miles. Then turn right onto a dirt road at a sign "Mount Zion Road 5510." In 0.1 mile, this road offers 3 routes. Park around here. (High clearance and four wheel drive cars can traverse the entire 6.7 miles of this road to the foot of Buckeye Peak when weather conditions permit.)

The Hike:

Follow the road going left (northwest) as it rises through the trees. Take the left fork at 0.25 miles and again at mile 0.8. Pass a radio tower at mile 1.3. At mile 4.3 you will be above timberline and reach Mount Zion. The summit cairn and a jar register will be a two minute side hike off the road to the right (east). Regain the road and continue north with some elevation loss over the rolling tundra. The trail bends northeast and rises between two unnamed peaks and ends at the foot of Buckeye Peak with Buckeye Lake down to the right (east). Follow the rocky ridge on the right to the north toward the summit which contains 3 separate U.S.G.S. markers and a ring of rocks around a cairn which supports a small metal tower. Return by way of your ascent route.

Buckeye Peak on far left and old mining road

167

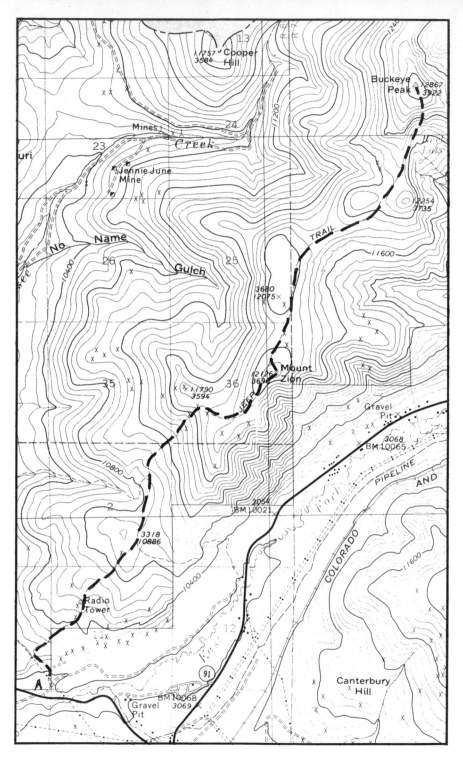

89. South Twin Cone Peak 12,323 feet

Hike Distance: 7.0 miles each way
Hiking Time: Up in 265 minutes. Down in 183 minutes.
Starting Elevation: 8,293 feet
Elevation Gain: 4,030 feet
Difficulty: More Difficult
Trail: All the way to the summit ridge
Relevant Maps: Mount Logan 7½ minute
                      Shawnee 7½ minute
                      Park County Number Two
                      Pike National Forest

Views from the summit: N to Mount Blaine and Mount Logan
                       NW to North Twin Cone Peak, Mount Bierstadt and
                       Mount Evans
                       SW to South Park
                       W to Kenosha Pass and Mount Guyot

Comment:

This is one of the Platte River Mountains and is visible from South Park around the town of Jefferson. Mount Blaine, one mile north, and North Twin Cone Peak, 1.3 miles northwest, can readily be reached over tundra and talus from this peak.

Directions to the trailhead:

On U.S. 285 drive either 2.1 miles west of the Shawnee Post Office or 2.7 miles east of the Camp Santa Maria entrance and park near a Ben Tyler Trail sign which is on the south side of the road.

The Hike:

Cross the road to the south where the trail begins and proceed up the gulch to the west southwest. In about 100 minutes take the left fork. In about 70 more minutes take the right fork to Rock Creek. Continue to ascend the gulch and in 24 more minutes reach the ridge and timberline. Then leave the trail and hike to your right (west) across marshes and scrub oak for about an hour past a false summit to a cairn and pole at the top. Descend by the same route.

South Twin Cone Peak from the east

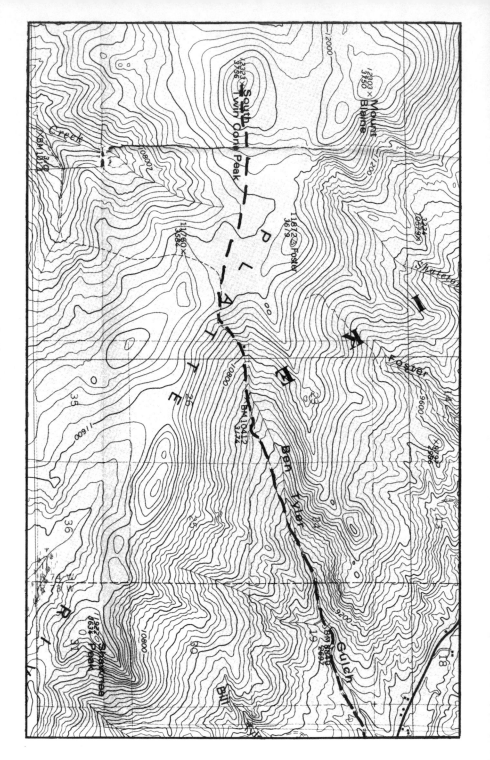

170

90. Antora Peak 13,269 feet

Hike Distance: 6.5 miles each way
Hiking Time: Up in 245 minutes. Down in 210 minutes.
Starting Elevation: 10,886 feet
Elevation Gain: 4,423 feet (includes 1,020 feet of extra elevation each way)
Difficulty: More Difficult
Trail: Initial 85%
Relevant Maps: Mount Ouray 7½ minute
Bonanza 7½ minute
Saguache County Number Two
San Isabel National Forest
Views from the summit: NNW to Chipeta Mountain and Mount Ouray
NNE to Sheep Mountain
NE to Porphyry Mountain
NW to Windy Peak
E to Bushnell Peak
SW to Sangre de Cristo Range
WSW to Mount Lindsey, Blanca Peak and
Little Bear Peak

Comment:

Marshall Pass was discovered by Army Lieutenant William L. Marshall, who was part of the Wheeler Survey team. The pass was first a wagon and then a railroad route between Gunnison and Salida. The first half of this hike is part of the Colorado Trail which will run from Denver to Durango when completed. The segment of this trail which is used for this hike generally parallels the Continental Divide. Many elk were seen by the author near timberline when he made this hike.

Directions to the trailhead:

From just west of Salida at the junction of U.S. 50 and U.S. 285, drive south toward Poncha Pass for 5.2 miles. Then turn right onto Chaffee County Road 200. This dirt road can be readily negotiated by regular cars all the way to Marshall Pass. Leaving U.S. 285 follow Chaffee County Road 200 for 2.35 miles and turn right into County Road 202. Ascend for 0.9 miles and turn right onto County Road 200 again. In 10.85 miles from U.S. 285 Marshall Pass (10,846 feet) will be reached. Just past the sign at the pass turn left and very quickly reach a 4 way intersection. Park around here. Marshall Pass can also be reached from the west via Sargents on U.S. 50.

The Hike:

Begin south on an excellent road which is part of the Colorado Trail. In about 5 minutes pass through a gate which blocks the road to vehicles. Antora Peak will be visible ahead. Lose some elevation and in about 25 minutes from the gate take the left fork which leads upward and generally south. Within 15 minutes you pass through a fence and encounter a trail sign. Continue south and in a mile reach signs which indicate that you are on the Divide Trail and that the Silver Creek Trail goes off and down to the east. The trail continues south and within another half hour cuts up into trees to pass through a barbed wire fence. Leave the main trail and follow this fence to the east directly toward Antora Peak. A faint trail passes alongside this fence at times. Within another half hour you will reach a gate through the fence and a definite trail leading south from the gate. Follow this trail as it curves around the western flank of Antora Peak. At a second creek crossing which will be reached in about twenty minutes, leave the trail and ascend to the east along the mostly dry creek bed up into a steep talus and snow filled gulch above timberline. Continue east over at times loose rock to a ridge which leads over a few false summits finally to a small cairn, an animal skull and two rock shelters at the top. For descent, take the same general route but take the ridge to your left. This ridge runs east to west and will enable you to descend over mostly tundra to reach the snow filled gulch at a lower level. Then continue back by way of your ascent route.

Antora Peak from the west

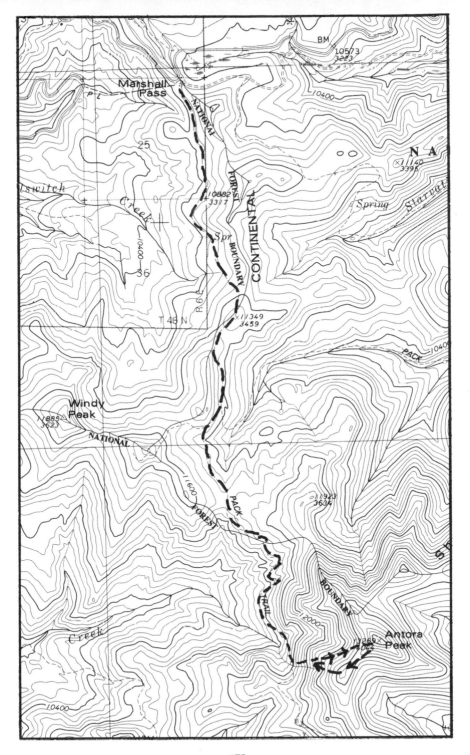

91. Mount Sopris 12,953 feet and West Mount Sopris 12,953 feet

Hike Distance: 6.0 miles each way
Hiking Time: Up in 285 minutes. Down in 225 minutes.
Starting Elevation: 8,600 feet
Elevation Gain: 5,089 feet (includes 736 feet of extra elevation gain between the two peaks and the false summit).
Difficulty: More Difficult
Trail: All the way
Relevant Maps: Mount Sopris 7½ minute
Basalt 7½ minute
Pitkin County Number One
White River National Forest
Views from the summit: E and W to the alternate summit
SE to Capitol Peak, Mount Daly and
Snowmass Mountain

Comment:

These two peaks are 0.8 miles apart and, interestingly, of identical height. Due to the absence of any nearby mountains of comparable height, Mount Sopris dominates the skyline as one looks southeast from the towns of Glenwood Springs and Carbondale. The mountain is named after Captain Richard Sopris who explored the area in 1860, discovered Glenwood Springs and later, in Denver, began City Park and became the mayor.

Directions to the trailhead:

Drive south on Colorado 133 from its junction with Colorado 82 at Carbondale for 2.8 miles and turn left onto a paved road with a stop sign. This is Colorado 111 which parallels Prince Creek up and to the southeast. After 1.6 miles on this road, take the right fork around where the pavement ends. Drive 4.8 miles further and again take a right fork. In 2.0 more miles you arrive at the trailhead and parking area. All vehicular access to the trail from this point is prevented by a barrier. (0.4 miles past the trailhead is road end at Dinkle Lake.)

The Hike:

Hike southeast and then south about 1.3 miles to a fork. The left route goes to Hay Park and West Sopris Creek. Take the right fork and go west and then southwest 2.0 more miles to the Thomas Lakes. From either the southeastern or the southwestern lake, a trail leads south up a steep but vegetated ridge. Take this route and keep to the left of the talus, pass timberline and rise to a ridge. Keep on the trail as it turns west (right) up the ridge and crosses a false summit en route to the Mount Sopris summit cairn. The West Mount Sopris lies 0.8 miles and about 30 minutes to the west over tundra and talus. There is a register and cairn at its summit. Follow the same trail back to the trailhead.

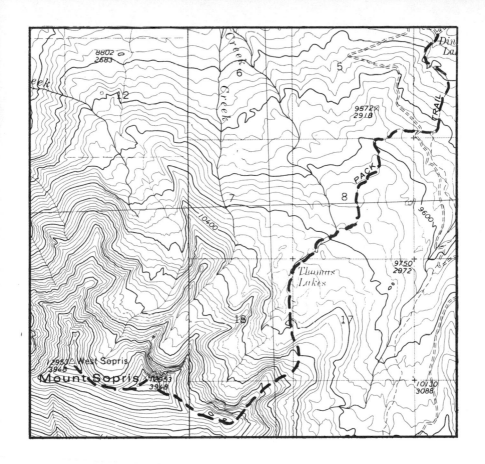

92. Iowa Peak 13,831 feet

Hike Distance: 7.0 miles each way
Hiking Time: Up in 298 minutes. Down in 197 minutes.
Starting Elevation: 9,669 feet
Elevation Gain: 4,962 feet (includes an extra 400 feet of elevation gain
                    each way)
Difficulty: More Difficult
Trail: Initial 80%
Relevant Maps: Winfield 7½ minute
                    Mount Harvard 7½ minute
                    Chaffee County Number One
                    San Isabel National Forest

Views from the summit: N to Missouri Mountain
                       ESE to Mount Harvard
                       S to Emerald Peak
                       SE to Mount Columbia
                       W to Huron Peak

Comment:

The ghost town of Vicksburg was occupied between 1881 and 1885. Named after Vick Keller, an early resident, the town once had two hotels and a school. Now only a small museum remains. Chaffee County is named after Jerome B. Chaffee one of the first two U.S. Senators from Colorado.

Directions to the trailhead:

Drive on U.S. 24 either 19.7 miles south from Leadville or 15.3 miles north from the traffic light in Buena Vista. Just south of the small settlement of Granite and just north of the Clear Creek Reservoir, a clearly marked dirt road, Chaffee County Road 390, goes 7.9 miles west to Vicksburg. At Vicksburg park in the fenced parking area on the south side of the road. Regular cars can come this far with no difficulty. (The road continues west southwest past Rockdale and Winfield to an eventual dead end.)

The Hike:

Follow the trail south from the parking area, cross Clear Creek on a bridge and soon, on the left, pass the grave of Baby Huffman, a miner's child who died at one month of age many years ago. Continue steeply up into Missouri Gulch on the trail which eventually runs alongside the creek. After one hour from the trailhead you will reach an abandoned cabin on your left. Continue up into the basin as two fourteeners come into view. These are Mount Belford on your left (east) and Missouri Mountain on your right (west). Continue on the trail above timberline and in about 130 minutes from the abandoned cabin you will reach Elkhead Pass at 13,220 feet. Ahead of you lies Missouri Basin and Mount Harvard. Iowa Peak will also come into view to the southwest with Emerald Peak on its left (south). Continue on the trail southward and down about four hundred feet from Elkhead Pass. Leave the trail whenever you see a clear gradual route to the Iowa Peak-Missouri Mountain saddle. The saddle will be reached in about 96 minutes from the pass. Then turn left (south) and ascend over easy tundra and talus in twelve minutes to the nondescript Iowa Peak summit. (Emerald Peak is an easy ridge walk to the south if you have the time and energy.) Descend by your ascent route.

Emerald Peak and Iowa Peak from Elkhead Pass

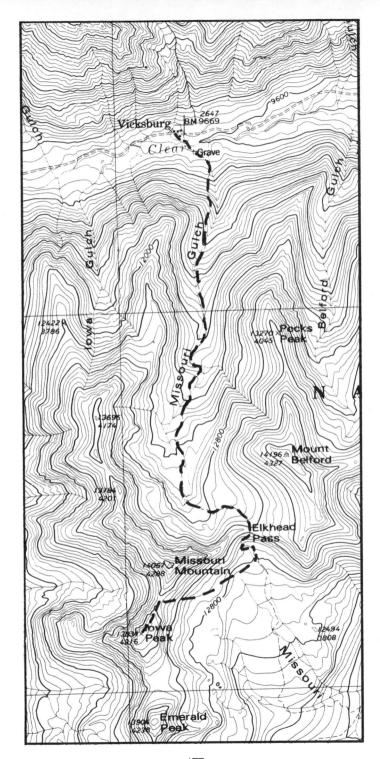

93. Engineer Mountain 13,218 feet

Hike Distance: 9.1 miles each way
Hiking Time: Up in 360 minutes. Down in 240 minutes.
Starting Elevation: 8,854 feet
Elevation Gain: 4,364 feet
Difficulty: Most Difficult
Trail: All the way
Relevant Maps: Handies Peak 7½ minute
                    Ouray County Number Two
                    San Juan County
                    Uncompahgre National Forest
Views from the summit: N to Engineer Pass, Coxcomb Peak, Uncompahgre
                    Peak and Wetterhorn Peak
                    NE to Dolly Varden Mountain
                    S to Houghton Mountain
                    SE to Handies Peak
                    W to Abrams Mountain

Comment:

Engineer Mountain is a name also given to other Colorado peaks. This peak lies just south of the Engineer Pass route which was built in 1877 by Otto Mears and carried stage coaches and wagons between Lake City on the east and Ouray and Silverton on the west. The original Engineer Pass was located closer to the Engineer Mountain summit and was steeper.

Directions to the trailhead:

Drive south from Ouray on U.S. 550 ("The Million Dollar Highway") for 3.4 miles to a cutoff to the east marked with a stop sign, an Ouray County Road 18 sign and an Engineer Mountain Road sign with recommendations for four wheel drive. Park here at the beginning of this road. (If you are able to drive your vehicle up this rough road, this will of course decrease the distances, times and elevation gain listed for this hike accordingly. High clearance is essential and four wheel drive will be needed on occasion.)

The Hike:

Proceed up the road and take the left fork at 2.3 miles. (The right fork leads into Poughkeepsie Gulch.) After 2.7 more miles again take the left fork. (The right fork goes to Mineral Point.) In 1.9 miles further continue again on the left fork. (The right fork leads south to Animas Forks and Cinnamon Pass.) By a series of switchbacks, you will reach the high point of this road in 1.9 miles from the last fork. At this highest point of the road, leave the main road and ascend to the east southeast via an old mining road for 0.3 miles to the summit which is marked by a metal rod embedded in a rock. Return as you ascended. (The main road which you left at its high point continues north for 0.4 miles to Engineer Pass and a large sign. The road continues down into Henson Gulch and ends in Lake City.)

Engineer Mountain from Engineer Pass

Coxcomb, Wetterhorn and Uncompahgre Peaks from Engineer Mountain

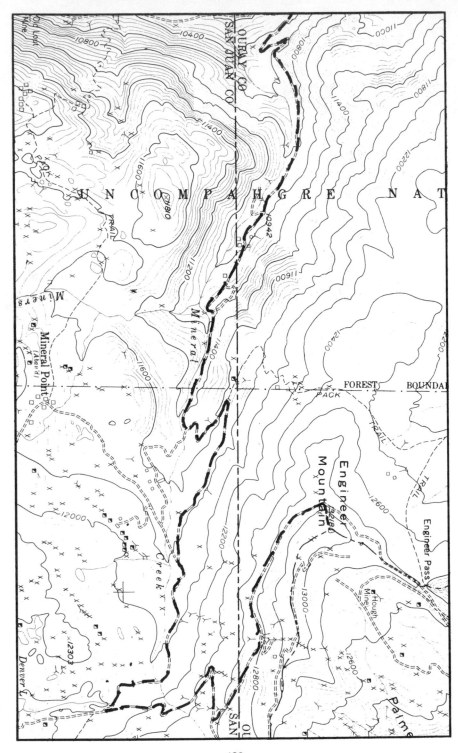

94. Pagoda Mountain 13,497 feet

Hike Distance: 6.2 miles each way
Hiking Time: Up in 375 minutes. Down in 278 minutes.
Starting Elevation: 8,380 feet
Elevation Gain: 5,117 feet
Difficulty: Most Difficult (due to length and elevation gain. No special danger).
Trail: The Sandbeach Lake Trail to Hunters Creek. Only intermittent and faint trail beyond. No trail from the creek junction to the summit.
Relevant Maps: Longs Peak 7½ minute
McHenrys Peak 7½ minute
Allens Park 7½ minute
Isolation Peak 7½ minute
Boulder County
Rocky Mountain National Park
Roosevelt National Forest
Views from the summit: N to Storm Peak
NE to Longs Peak
E to Mount Meeker
W to Chiefs Head Peak
WNW to McHenrys Peak and the Spearhead.

Comment:

Pagoda Mountain is named after the prominent configuration of its summit which can be seen on clear days from the Boulder and Denver areas as the peak to the left of Longs Peak. Although this mountain and most of the hike described lies with Rocky Mountain National Park, no park fee is required for access to this trail.

Directions to the trailhead:

Drive 2.2 miles north of Allenspark or 1.1 miles south of Meeker Park on Colorado 7 and take the paved road going southwest to the Wild Basin Ranger Station. Drive 0.4 miles and make a right turn onto a dirt road to Copeland Lake and the Wild Basin Ranger Station. Park in the designated area within 100 yards on your right. This is the Sandbeach Lake Trailhead and your starting point.

The Hike:

Proceed northwest to the right of Copeland Lake for 100 yards to a sign and the Sandbeach Lake Trailhead. The trail begins steeply to the northwest and then curves west for about 3.0 miles to where Hunters Creek crosses the trail flowing from the northwest. This junction will be reached in about 90 minutes. Leave the Sandbeach Lake Trail and angle obliquely to the northwest following Hunters Creek keeping it on your left. After about 1.3 miles along Hunters Creek you will reach a junction of two branches of the creek. Cross this junction, continue northwest and leave the creeks. Stay close to the base of Mount Meeker which lies to your right. Pagoda Mountain will now be visible. Continue eventually in a more northerly direction, often over rocks up into a couloir with talus and scree and some loose footing to the saddle which lies to the east (right) of Pagoda Mountain and to the left of Longs Peak. From the saddle turn west and ascend steeply over boulders to a summit cairn and a register cylinder. Some easy hand work is necessary between the saddle and the top but the footing is quite solid. Return the same way you ascended.

Pagoda Mountain—Longs Peak saddle from the south

Pagoda Mountain from the trough on Longs Peak

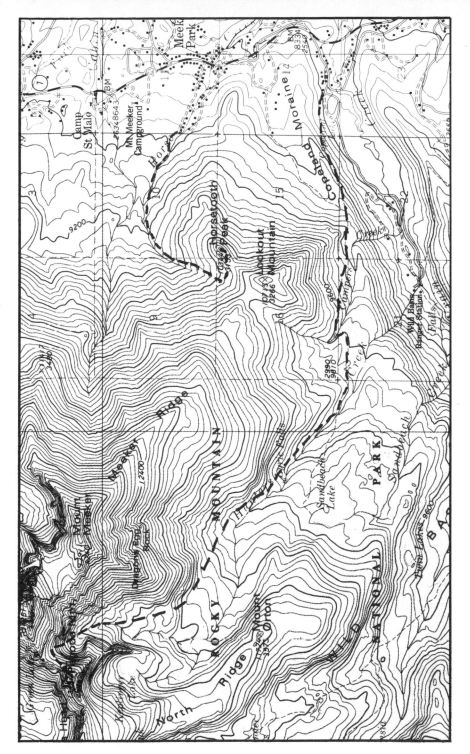

95. Capitol Peak 14,130 feet

Hike Distance: 8.12 miles each way
Hiking Time: Day 1: 197 minutes up to base camp. Day 2: Up in 218 minutes. Down to base camp in 188 minutes. Base camp to car in 162 minutes.
Starting Elevation: 9,420 feet
Elevation Gain: 5,660 feet. Day 1: − 2,660 feet. Day 2: − 3,000 feet. (Includes 475 feet of extra elevation gain each way.)
Difficulty: Most Difficult (due to overall length and elevation gain. Considerable hand work necessary after K-2)
Trail: All the way
Relevant Maps: Capitol Peak 7½ minute
Pitkin County Number One
White River National Forest
Views from the summit: N to Capitol Lake
NNE to Mount Daly
NW to Mount Sopris
E to Clark Peak and the Pierre Lakes
SE to Snowmass Mountain

Comment:

This is the most strenuous hike in this guide but also the most spectacular. Capitol Peak and nearby Snowmass Mountain were called "The Twins" or the "Capitol" and the "Whitehouse" by earlier residents of the area.

Directions to the trailhead:

Drive north from the Castle Creek bridge in Aspen on Colorado 82 for 13.8 miles or drive south from Glenwood Springs on Colorado 82 for 23 miles. At the Snowmass Post Office and a service station on the south side of the road turn south along Snowmass Creek for 1.8 miles to a T. Turn right and drive southwest. After 4.9 miles from the T, the road paving ends. Continue on the dirt road for 3.4 more miles to the road end in a grove of trees. A sign marks the trail on your left. Park here.

The Hike:

There is a lovely view of Capitol Peak at the end of the basin from the trailhead. Hike down and south on the excellent trail. You will lose 380 feet en route to a crossing of Capitol Creek over a large tree trunk. The trail then rises and crosses Capitol Creek a few more times. The trail is not steadily upward and you will occasionally lose some altitude. After more than 6 miles you arrive at a flat, tree covered area just at timberline to the right of the trail. This makes a good camp site. Several hundred yards further south lies Capitol Lake which often stays frozen well into July.

The next morning continue south on the trail which forks and continue steeply up and east to the saddle between Mt. Daly on the left and Capitol Peak on the right. From this saddle, the trail proceeds south along the eastern flanks of the Capitol Peak ridge. The trail at this point is marked by cairns and follows a series of ledges. Some use of hands may be necessary but the exposure is slight. Eventually a talus slope is reached. Cross this to gain the summit of a subpeak at 13,664 feet, called K-2.

The Capitol Peak summit will now be visible to the southwest across a rocky ridge. Descend from K-2 toward this ridge, part of which is known as "The Knife Edge." This area, about 60 feet long, is best traversed by straddling. The rock is solid but the drop-offs on your right and left are quite abrupt and lengthy. In good weather, this crossing can readily be made. The trail then continues by way of cairn marked ledges in a clockwise direction to a summit cairn and a register cylinder. Your only choice on return is to avoid the rocky ledges between K-2 and the Mt. Daly—K-2 saddle by going more easterly from the K-2 summit into the snowfields and then going north to reach the Mt. Daly—K-2 saddle. An ice axe will be needed here. The snowfield route is the easier. From the saddle the way down is the clear trail which brought you up.

Capitol Peak from the north

The knife edge and ridge to the Capitol Peak summit

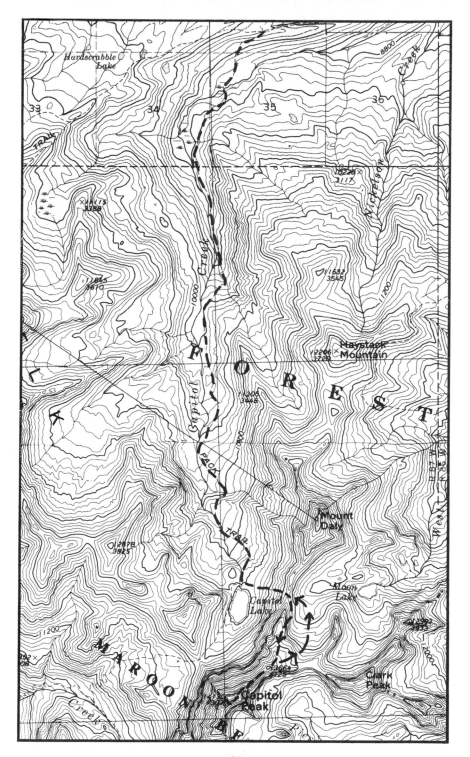

REFERENCES

1. Aldrich, John K. *Ghosts of Park County: A Guide To The Ghost Towns and Mining Camps of Park County.* Lakewood, Colorado; Centennial Graphics, 1984.
2. Boddie, Caryn and Boddie, Peter. *The Hiker's Guide to Colorado.* Billings, Montana; Falcon Press Publishing Company, Inc. 1984.
3. Borneman, Walter R. and Lampert, Lyndon L. *A Climbing Guide To Colorado's Fourteeners.* Boulder, Colorado; Pruett Publishing Company, 1978.
4. Borneman, Walter R. *Colorado's Other Mountains.* Evergreen, Colorado; Cordillera Press, Inc. 1984.
5. Brown, Robert L. *Uphill Both Ways.* Caldwell, Idaho; The Caxton Printers, Ltd. 1976.
6. Dallas, Sandra. *Colorado Ghost Towns and Mining Camps.* Norman, Oklahoma; University of Oklahoma Press, 1985.
7. Dannen, Kent and Dannen, Donna. *Rocky Mountain National Park Hiking Trails.* Charlotte, North Carolina; East Woods Press Books, 1978.
8. Dawson, J. Frank. *Place Names in Colorado.* Denver, Colorado; The J. Frank Dawson Publishing Company, 1954.
9. Eichler, George R. *Colorado Place Names.* Boulder, Colorado; Johnson Publishing Co., 1977.
10. Ellis, Erl and Ellis, Carrie S. *The Saga Of Upper Clear Creek.* Frederick, Colorado; Jende-Hagan Book Corporation, 1983.
11. Garratt, Mike and Martin, Bob. *Colorado's High Thirteeners.* Evergreen, Colorado; Cordillera Press, Inc. 1984.
12. Gilliland, Mary E. *The Summit Hiker.* Silverthorne, Colorado; Alpenrose Press, 1983.
13. Hagen, Mary. *Hiking Trails of Northern Colorado.* Boulder, Colorado; Pruett Publishing Company, 1979.
14. Hill, Alice Polk. *Colorado Pioneers In Picture And Story.* Denver, Colorado; Brock-Haffner Press, 1915.
15. Koch, Don. *The Colorado Pass Book.* Boulder, Colorado; Pruett Publishing Company, 1980.
16. Kramarsic, Joseph D. *Bibliography of Colorado Mountain Ascents 1863-1976.* Dillon, Colorado; Self Published, 1979.
17. LaBaw, Wallace L. *God, Gold, Girls and Glory.* Broomfield Colorado; Ingersoll Publications, 1966.
18. Lowe, Don and Lowe, Roberta. *80 Northern Colorado Hiking Trails.* Beaverton, Oregon; The Touchstone Press, 1973.
19. Mahoney, Stanley. *Mount Evans Above Timberline.* Westminster, Colorado; Self Published, 1970.
20. Mahoney, Stan and Mahoney, Martha. *Roads and Trails and Timberline Snails.* Boulder, Colorado; Johnson Publishing Company, 1972.
21. Martin, Bob. *Hiking Trails of Central Colorado.* Boulder, Colorado; Pruett Publishing Company, 1983.
22. Martin, Bob. *Hiking the Highest Passes.* Boulder, Colorado; Pruett Publishing Company, 1984.
23. Ormes, Robert M. *Guide To The Colorado Mountains.* Colorado Springs, Colorado; Self Published, Eighth Edition, 1983.
24. Ringrose, Linda W. and Rathbun, Linda M. *Foothills To Mount Evans.* Evergreen, Colorado; The Wordsmiths, 1980.

INDEX

INDEX

INDEX

INDEX

INDEX

INDEX

INDEX

INDEX

ORDER FORM

DJM ENTERPRISES
Post Office Box 61332
Denver, Colorado 80206

Please send me _____ copies of **Colorado Mountain Hikes For Everyone** at **$11.95** each. Coloradans: Please add 7% sales tax. Shipping: $1 for the first book and 50 cents for each additional book.

Please allow 3-4 weeks for delivery.

ORDER FORM

DJM ENTERPRISES
Post Office Box 61332
Denver, Colorado 80206

Please send me _____ copies of **Colorado Mountain Hikes For Everyone** at **$11.95** each. Coloradans: Please add 7% sales tax. Shipping: $1 for the first book and 50 cents for each additional book.

Please allow 3-4 weeks for delivery.